10 Minute Guide to
Q&A™

Arlene Azzarello

SAMS

A Division of Macmillan Computer Publishing
11711 North College, Carmel, Indiana 46032 USA

To the memory of Bonnie Hontas.

International Standard Book Number: 0-672-22832-7
Library of Congress Catalog Card Number: 90-64348

Acquisitions Editor: *Marie Butler-Knight*
Book Design: *Dan Armstrong, reVisions Plus, Inc.*
Manuscript Editors: *reVisions Plus, Inc.*
Cover Design: *Dan Armstrong*
Production: *reVisions Plus, Inc.*
Indexer: *Katherine Murray*
Technical Reviewer: *San Dee Phillips*
Printed in the United States of America.

Trademarks

All terms mentioned in this book that are known to be trademarks or service marks are listed below. In addition, terms suspected are capitalized. SAMS cannot attest to the accuracy of this information. Use of a term in this book should not be regarded as affecting the validity of any trademark or service mark.

Q&A is a trademark of Symantec Corporation.

1-2-3, Lotus, and Symphony are registered trademarks of Lotus Development Corporation

dBASE is a registered trademark of Ashton-Tate.

Paradox is a registered trademark of Ansa Corporation

PFS is a registered trademark and Professional Write is a trademark of Software Publishing Corporation.

Contents

Introduction

Q&A is an integrated database and word processing program that lets you organize, store, retrieve, manipulate, and print information with a computer. You can design a form as simple as the printed ones in the address book that you use to keep track of the names, addresses, and telephone numbers of your friends and business associates. Or you can design complex forms to organize and impose consistency over a large range of business data—both textual and numeric. With Q&A you can also

- Enter and update information in a consistent manner

- Look at all or parts of your stored information

- Make reports and calculations using your stored data

- Write letters, memos, and documents with Write, Q&A's word processor

- Create and print mass mailings, invoices, and mailing labels

- Import data from other database and spreadsheet programs

- Customize Q&A's menus and make custom help screens to suit your own needs or the requirements of your business

- Program and automate stored procedures such as specifications for retrieving data or generating reports that must be produced on a regular or frequent basis

The *10 Minute Guide to Q&A* assumes that

- You need to learn the program quickly

- You need to identify and learn only the tasks necessary to accomplish this goal

- You need some clear-cut, simple-English help to learn about the basic features of the program

If you have little time but your career demands that you get results from new software *quickly*, the *10 Minute Guide* will lead you through the most important features of the program in a simple, "no-frills" format.

Because you probably don't have hours of uninterrupted time to sit and learn a new program, the *10 Minute Guide* teaches you the operations you need in lessons you can complete in 10 minutes or less. Not only does the 10-minute format offer information in small, easy-to-follow modules (making operations easy to learn and remember), it enables you to stop and start as often as you like, because each lesson is a self-contained series of steps it takes to perform a particular task.

What Are the *10 Minute Guides*?

The *10 Minute Guide* series is a new approach to learning computer programs. Instead of trying to teach everything about a particular software product, the *10 Minute Guides* teach you only about the most often-used features in a particular program. Organized in lesson format, each *10 Minute Guide* contains between 20 and 30 short lessons.

You'll find only simple English explaining the procedures in this book. With straightforward steps and special artwork (called *icons*), the *10 Minute Guides* make learning a new software program easy and fast.

The following icons help you find your way around in the *10 Minute Guide to Q&A.*

 Timesaver Tips offer shortcuts and hints for using the program effectively.

 Plain English icons identify definitions of new terms.

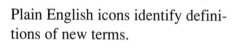 Panic Button icons appear at places where new users often run into trouble.

A table of features at the end of the book provides you with a quick guide to Q&A options that are not given full coverage in the lessons. You can use this table either as a reference for more information or as a quick guide to finding the menus and options for performing routine operations.

Specific conventions in this book help you find your way around Q&A as easily as possible:

What you type   The information you type or select appears in bold type and in color.

Menu, option, field, and key names	Menu names, the names of options or fields, and the names of keyboard keys appear with the first letter capitalized.
`What you see on the screen`	Characters you see on your screen appear in computer type.

Who Should Use the *10 Minute Guide to Q&A?*

The *10 Minute Guide to Q&A* is the answer for those who:

- Need to learn Q&A quickly.

- Don't have a lot of time to spend learning a new program.

- Feel overwhelmed by the complexity of the Q&A program.

- Are new computer users intimidated by learning new programs.

- Want to find out whether Q&A will meet their database management, reporting, and word processing needs.

- Want a clear, concise guide to the most important features of the Q&A program.

Whether you are a manager, accountant, member of an office support staff, a lawyer, a teacher, business owner, or simply a budding computer novice, the *10 Minute Guide to Q&A* will help you find and learn the most important aspects of the Q&A program as quickly as possible. If your time is important to you and you need to make the most of it, you will find that the *10 Minute Guide to Q&A* helps you learn this incredibly popular—and   powerful—program in a fraction of the time you might ordinarily spend struggling with new software.

What Is in This Book?

The *10 Minute Guide to Q&A* consists of a series of lessons, ranging from basic startup to a few more advanced features. Remember, however, that nothing in this book is difficult. Although most users will want to start at the beginning of the book and progress through the lessons sequentially, you can complete the lessons in any order.

If Q&A has not been installed on your computer, consult the inside front cover for installation steps. If you need to review basic DOS commands for preparing diskettes, see the "DOS Primer" at the back of this book.

This book concludes with a Table of Features that provides you with the menus and selections you can use to access the features.

For Further Reference...

Look for these other SAMS books that will add to your knowledge of Q&A:

- *The First Book of Q&A 4.0,* by Sandra Eddy.

- *Q&A in Business,* by David Adams.

Acknowledgments

Heartfelt thanks to the following individuals and organizations for all their help and support during the preparation of this book: Marie Butler-Knight, Cimage Corporation, Sam Eudaly, Erik Heuer, Jean Jacobson, Katherine Murray, Beth Nagengast, Amy Perry, Dave Reid, reVisions Plus, Norman Roth, John Russo, SAMS, Eva Story, Pete Story, Symantec Corporation, Estelle Taylor, and Jane Vaden.

Arlene Azzarello
Los Altos Hills, California

Lesson 1

Getting Started

In this lesson, you'll learn how to start and quit Q&A, select options from Q&A's menus, and navigate through the menu structure.

Starting Q&A

Before you can start Q&A, the program must be installed on your computer (see installation instructions on the inside front cover), and the drive and directory in which Q&A is installed must be the current directory (such as C:\QA).

To make C:\QA the current directory, follow these steps:

1. At the DOS prompt, type C:.

2. Press Enter.

3. Type CD\QA.

4. Press Enter.

See the "DOS Primer" at the back of this book for more information on the CD command and other DOS commands.

1

DOS Confusion Be careful with spaces when you are using DOS commands. If you omit a space or add one too many, DOS may display an error message.

To start Q&A, simply type **QA** and press Enter. The program displays a title screen, and then a screen containing Q&A's Main Menu is displayed, as shown in Figure 1-1.

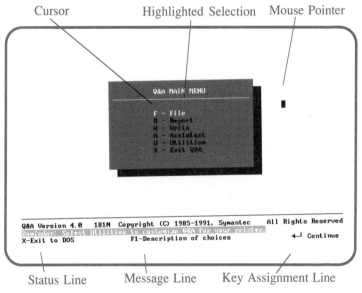

Figure 1-1. Q&A's Main Menu.

 Menu-Driven Program Q&A is a *menu-driven* program, which means it provides lists of options from which you can choose. You don't have to enter special commands to instruct the program what to do next.

The Q&A Main Menu Screen

The options on the Main Menu are

2

- **F - File** for designing and maintaining a database and retrieving information from it

- **R - Report** for designing, formatting, and printing reports of information in a database

- **W - Write** for writing, editing, formatting, and printing documents and mailing labels

- **A - Assistant** for running Q&A by typing simple English instructions for Q&A's Intelligent Assistant

- **U - Utilities** for installing printers, maintaining DOS files, and installing alternate programs

- **X - Exit Q&A** for quitting Q&A

Notice the *status line* in Figure 1-1. The status line appears near the bottom of the screen and provides reminders, status information about file names and record numbers, and special prompts that tell you what to do next.

At the very bottom of the screen, Q&A displays a *key assignment line* listing important keys that you can use. For example, from the Main Menu screen you can press

F1   To display a help screen containing a
        description of each Main Menu option

Enter   To continue by selecting an option

X   To quit Q&A altogether

Selecting Menu Options

You can select options from Q&A menus using either the keyboard or a mouse. Selecting an option involves highlighting it and then activating it.

To select an option by using the keyboard:

1. Press the ↑ and ↓ keys to move the highlight to the option you want.

2. Press F10 or Enter (whichever appears on the key assignment line).

Or

1. Press the letter or number key given for the option you want. For example, press **F** for the **File** option.

2. Press F10 or Enter.

To select an option by using the mouse:

1. Move the mouse until the mouse pointer is over the option you want.

2. Click the left mouse button.

Click means press and release the left mouse button.

Setting Automatic Execution The makers of Q&A recommend that you activate the automatic execution utility so that you can select a menu option by pressing only the letter or number key for the option, without F10 or Enter. To activate automatic execution, select **U - Utilities** from the Main Menu, **S - Set global options** from the Utilities Menu, and **Yes** next to **Automatic Execution:** on the Set Global Options Menu.

Moving among Menus

When you select a Q&A option, the program displays another menu giving additional choices or prompts you to enter information. Each new menu appears in front of and slightly offset from the previous menu (see Figure 1-2). This capability lets you see at all times how many menus you've called up since the Main Menu.

To return to the previous menu by using the keyboard:

- Press Esc.

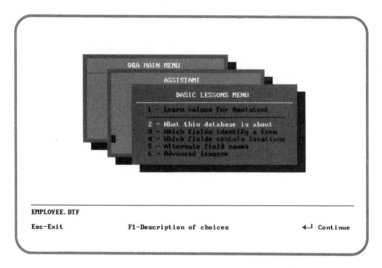

Figure 1-2. Submenus off the Main Menu.

To return to the previous menu by using the mouse:

- Move the mouse pointer outside the current menu box and click the left mouse button.

  Or

- Move the mouse pointer over Esc in the key assignment line and click the left mouse button.

5

To return all the way to the Main Menu, repeat these steps until only the Main Menu appears on the screen.

Quitting Q&A

To end a Q&A session, simply select **X - Exit Q&A** from the Main Menu. Do *not* turn off your computer to end a session: You risk losing or damaging your data if you do.

In this lesson, you've learned to start and quit a Q&A session. The next lesson introduces you to the Q&A database.

Lesson 2

Overview of a Q&A Database

In this lesson, you'll learn basic database terms and find out how to access the Q&A help screens. You'll also use the Intelligent Assistant to load and view records in form and table views.

Getting Help from Q&A

Help screens are available throughout Q&A. They provide information on the options available from a menu or the type of entry Q&A expects from you. Figure 2-1 shows a sample help screen. To display the help screen for the current menu,

- Press F1.

To return to the menu when you are finished reading the help screen,

- Press Esc.

Basic Database Concepts

A *database* is a collection of information that you have stored. It consists of a *form* (the fundamental layout that

7

defines the organization of your information) and *records* (the actual information you insert into the form). A form, like the printed form in an address book, contains named *fields* that are the areas in which you can enter information. For example, each record consists of the related data entered in the fields, such as the name, address, and phone number of an individual in your address book.

CHOICE	DESCRIPTION	VOLUME
File	Create, fill out, and work with forms of information.	1
Report	Take information from your records, sort and arrange it, and print results in a table or a Cross Tab.	1
Write	Write and print documents.	2
Assistant	Teach your Intelligent Assistant (IA) and Query Guide about your records then ask questions, generate reports or change information in English.	1
Utilities	Set-up your printer, modify font files, setup alternate programs, DOS file facilities, etc.	2

CAUTION: Sudden loss or interruption of power can damage a data file. Never turn your machine off or reboot the system UNLESS you are at one of the main Q&A menus. However, if a power loss does occur, you can probably recover the file (see pg. U-65). Make frequent backups (pg. F-193).

Figure 2-1. Help screen for the Q&A Main Menu.

The database form and records are stored by your computer in different files. A *file* is simply a unit of storage; it is the electronic equivalent of a traditional file folder.

First Look at a Database

The easiest way to get acquainted with a Q&A database is to use Q&A's Intelligent Assistant and Query Guide to load records and view the data in them. To do so, follow these steps:

1. Select **A - Assistant** from the Main Menu.

2. When Q&A displays the Assistant Menu (shown in Figure 2-2), select **Q - Query Guide.**

3. With the cursor in the File Name: box at the bottom of the screen, press Enter. A list of files available in the QA directory appears, as shown in Figure 2-3.

4. From the list of files, select **EMPLOYEE.DTF**, one of Q&A's built-in, sample databases. The Query Guide option list appears, as shown in Figure 2-4.

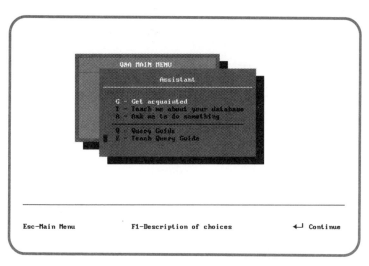

Figure 2-2. The Assistant Menu.

Viewing Records in Form View

The Query Guide has options that let you run Q&A by constructing statements in English. To build a sentence to display all the records in the database follow these steps:

1. From the list of options Q&A provides, select **F** - Find ... (records)

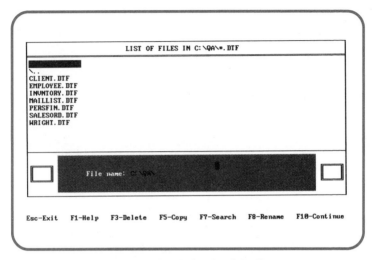

Figure 2-3. Files available in the QA directory.

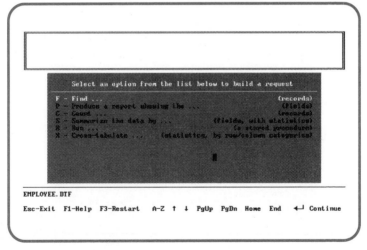

Figure 2-4. Query Guide option list.

2. Notice that Q&A displays the word **Find** in the request box at the top of the screen to remind you of the request you've built so far.

3. Select A - ALL the records ... .

4. Select . - . [to execute the command].

Q&A displays the EMPLOYEE.DTF form and the data in its first record, as shown in Figure 2-5. The cursor is in the first field of the form. This screen is displayed in *form view*.

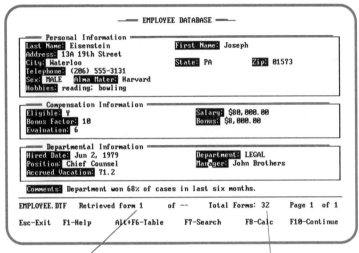

Number of the Record You're Viewing   Total Number of Records in the Database

Figure 2-5. Sample record displayed in form view.

Press F10 to display the data in the second record in the database. Q&A displays the number of the record you're viewing and the total number of records in the database at the bottom of the screen. You can press F10 to step through each record and view the data in each of their fields.

Viewing Records in Table View

Instead of looking at the data one record at a time, you can display all the data in the database in *table view* as shown in Figure 2-6. To activate table view,

11

• Press Alt and F6 simultaneously.

Record   Field

Last Name	First Name	Address	City	State
Eisenstein	Joseph	13A 19th Street	Waterloo	PA
Jacobson	Will	420 Selby Lane	Atherton	CA
Jeffers	David	1532 Broadway	Boston	MA
Gallway	James	23 Embarcadero	Daley City	CA
Guy	Mary	411 Pine Street	Boston	MA
Robertson	Randolph	879 Freeway Bl→	Culver City	CA
Darwin	Charles	5 Gullapagus W→	Big Turtle	PA
Stoleman	Robert	1056 Hall Stre→	Santa Monica	CA
Johnson	Charles	7677 Lucky Dri→	Boise	ID
Criswell	Ernest	278 Glencoe	Boston	MA
Rutledge	Nina	2934 Underwood→	Boston	MA
Stack	David	1532 Broadway	Boston	MA
Lapuz	Janice	47 Wilburn St.	Savannah	GA
Brothers	John	234 Big Tree L→	Pittsburgh	PA
Phips	Alphonse	127 Bearcroft →	Columbia	SC
Gyorfi	Natalia	15 West St.	San Francisco	CA
Johnson	Mildred	15 Broadway	San Francisco	CA

EMPLOYEE.DTF   Retrieved record 2   of --   Total records: 32

Esc-Exit F1-Help { ↓ ↑ → ← Home End PgUp PgDn }-Navigate   F10-Show form

Figure 2-6. Sample records in table view.

The data for each record in the database appears in a single *row* in table view. Each field in the database form is a *column* in table view.

Notice that Q&A's key assignment line at the bottom of the screen reminds you which keys you can use. You can move the highlight through the rows and columns of the table with any of these keys. Alternatively, you can position the mouse pointer over a field you want to see and click the left mouse button.

Fields that contain more data than can be displayed on a monitor end with a right arrow. To view the rest of the data in such a field:

• Press F6.

Q&A displays all of the data in the field in the Field Editor window at the bottom of the screen. To return to table view,

● Press F10.

This sample database contains more fields and records than can be displayed on the screen at one time. Check the key assignment line at the bottom of the screen for the keys you can press to move the display from field to field and record to record. Experiment with these keys to see how they help you navigate through the database in table view. These keys are summarized in Table 2-1.

Table 2-1. Keys for Navigating in Table View.

Key	Action
↓ Arrow	Moves down to next record in same field
↑Arrow	Moves up to next record in same field
→ Arrow	Moves right to next field of same record
← Arrow	Moves left to next field of same record
Home	Moves to top of screen in same field
End	Moves to bottom of screen in same field
Page Up	Moves up 17 records
Page Down	Moves down 17 records

In this lesson, you've seen a sample database and learned the basic terms associated with it. You've also learned the difference between the form view and the table view, and how to move about in the table view. These concepts will be explored in more detail in later lessons.

Lesson 3

Creating a
Simple Form

In this lesson, you'll learn to create a simple form that you can use to build a database.

Planning Your Form

Just as you would plan a form like the printed ones in an address book, making a pencil sketch of how you want your database form to appear on the monitor can save you some time. At a minimum, your sketch should include:

- Field labels (the names you want to assign to fields)

- Field sizes (a rough estimate of the space required for data entry in each field)

The Form Design Screen

To start designing a form, follow these steps:

1. Start Q&A by following the instructions in Lesson 1.

2. Select **F - File** from the Main Menu and **D - Design a new file** from the File Menu.

3. Q&A displays the Data file: box at the bottom of the screen, as shown in Figure 3-1. Type a name (containing no more than eight alphanumeric characters) for your database file and press Enter.

4. Q&A adds a `.DTF` extension to the name and displays the blank Form Design screen shown in Figure 3-2.

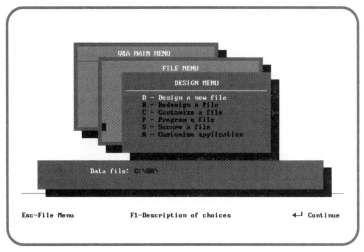

Figure 3-1. The Design Menu with Data file: box.

When you make entries, a bright rectangle moves across the ruler at the bottom of the screen, showing the current horizontal cursor position. Beneath the ruler, Q&A displays a line number indicating the current vertical position of the cursor.

Designing the Form

To design your form, you'll type a label for each field and define its size. A field *label* contains

- The name of the field

- A : (colon) or a < (left angle bar)

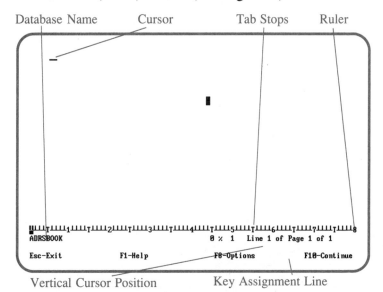

Database Name   Cursor   Tab Stops   Ruler

ADRSBOOK

Esc-Exit   F1-Help   F8-Options   F10-Continue

Vertical Cursor Position   Key Assignment Line

Figure 3-2. A blank Form Design screen.

The colon or left angle bar separates the field label from the actual field. Q&A displays the colon as part of the field label when you use the form later to add data; the left angle bar is displayed as a blank.

To define the size of a field, you simply specify where the field ends. Position the cursor at the end of the field, and then

- Type > (right angle bar).

  Or

- Press Enter.

For example, Figure 3-3 shows entries for an address book form. Figure 3-4 illustrates how Q&A displays those entries when you're adding data.

Single-line Field   Field Label **[for left angle bar]**

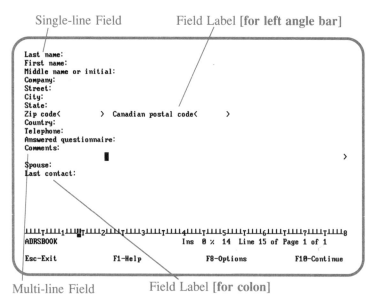

Multi-line Field   Field Label **[for colon]**

Figure 3-3. Sample entries for an address book form.

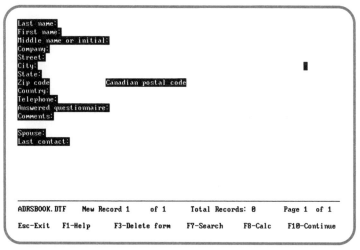

Figure 3-4. Q&A's display of a sample address book form.

When you finish typing field labels and defining field sizes, press F10 to save your form design.

Correcting Mistakes If you make a mistake, move the cursor with the mouse or the arrow keys, and type over it. You can also press Backspace or Delete to remove unwanted entries.

Specifying Information Types for Fields

After you save a form design, Q&A displays the design in a Format Spec screen as illustrated in Figure 3-5. This screen shows you that Q&A automatically assigned a text information type (denoted by a **T**) to each field you defined.

Information Type The *information type* determines the kind of data that you can enter in a field and how you can process that data.

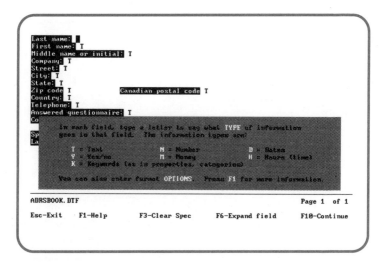

Figure 3-5. The Format Spec screen.

Text fields accept alphanumeric characters and punctuation. You can sort textual records alphabetically. If you give a field a number information type (denoted by an **N**), it accepts only numerals. You can perform calculations on numeric records and sort them numerically. Table 3-1 summarizes Q&A's information types.

Table 3-1. Q&A Information Types.

Code	Type	Information
D	Dates	Dates
H	Hours	Times
K	Keyword	Unique words or codes for which you can search
M	Money	Currency
N	Number	Numeric data used in calculations
T	Text	Alphanumeric characters and punctuation
Y	Yes/No	Responses to yes/no or true/false questions

You can specify a field's information type and set formatting options at the same time.

Formatting Options These options control the display of data entered in an individual field.

Press F1 to display the help screen shown in Figure 3-6. This screen summarizes the alignment and typographical options available for each information type.

To set field information types and formatting options:

1. Press Esc to return to the Format Spec screen.

19

2. Move the cursor to the field.

3. Type the code for the information type followed by a , (comma), and then add formatting codes separated by commas.

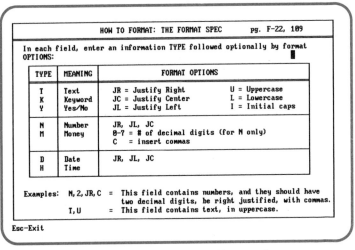

Figure 3-6. How to Format: The Format Spec screen.

4. Repeat steps 2 and 3 until you've finished making your specifications, and then press F10.

Global Formatting Options

Global formatting options control the display of *all* data entered in date, hour, money, and number fields. When you press F10 after specifying these information types and format options, Q&A displays the Global Format Options screen shown in Figure 3-7. To change a global formatting option:

1. Move the highlight to the name of the option by using the mouse or the arrow keys.

2. Select the option you want.

3. Repeat steps 1 and 2 until you've finished.

4. Press F10 to save your form design with your formatting specifications and return to the File Menu.

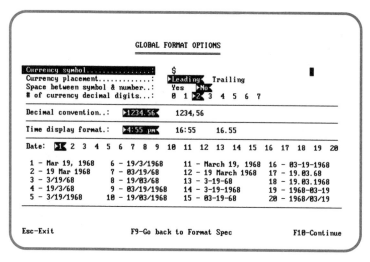

Figure 3-7. The Global Format Options screen.

In this lesson, you've learned the basic steps required to design a database form. Changing a design is covered in Lesson 9. In the next lesson, you'll enter information in a database.

Entering
Information
in a Database

In this lesson, you'll learn how to add, save, and edit
the data in your database.

The Data Entry Screen

Once you've designed a database form, you can load it as
follows:

1. Start Q&A.

2. Select **F - File** from the Main Menu and **A - Add
   data** from the File Menu.

3. With the cursor in the File Name: box at the bottom
   of the screen, press the space bar and then press
   Enter.

4. Select the name of your database file from the list
   that Q&A displays.

Q&A retrieves your database form and displays a blank
copy of it on the screen. As shown in Figure 4-1, the status
line indicates the number Q&A will assign to the first
record you'll add, the total number of records *for this
session*, and the total number of records in the database.
The form's current page number and the total number of

pages in the form are shown on the far right of the status line.

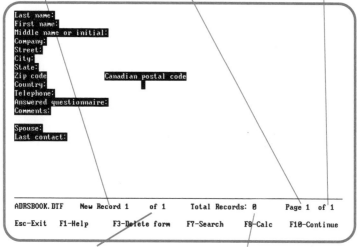

New Record Number   Current Page Number   Total Records in Database

Total Records for this Session   Total Number of Pages in Form

Figure 4-1. The ADRSBOOK.DTF blank form.

Moving among Fields

When Q&A displays a blank form ready for data entry, the cursor is in the first field. You can move the cursor to another field by positioning the mouse pointer in it and clicking the left mouse button. You can also move the cursor from the keyboard. Table 4-1 summarizes the keys used to move among fields.

Table 4-1. Keys for Moving among Fields when Adding Data.

Key	Action
Enter	Moves to next field
Tab	Moves to next field

continued

23

Table 4-1. (continued)

Key	Action
↓ Arrow	Moves *down* to next field
↑Arrow	Moves *up* to next field
Shift+Tab	Moves to previous field
Home	Moves to first field in form
End	Moves to last field in form

Entering and Saving Data

To add a record to your database:

1. Fill in the blank form by typing in your information in the appropriate fields.

Correcting Errors If you make a mistake before you press F10, you can move the cursor to the error and type over it. You can also press Delete or Backspace to remove unwanted characters.

2. Press F10 to save the record and display another blank form.

3. Repeat step 2 until you want to end a session.

4. To end a session and return to the File Menu, press Shift and F10 simultaneously.

Removing Error Messages If you press F10 when a blank form is displayed, Q&A issues an error message on the status line. Press Esc to remove this message and return to the File Menu.

If you have more information than will fit in a field as it was defined, you can expand the field by pressing F6.

24

Q&A displays its Field Editor window superimposed on the form, as shown in Figure 4-2. Any characters you've already typed are shown in the window.

Field Editor Window

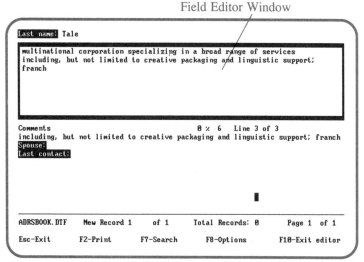

Figure 4-2. The Field Editor window.

You can continue typing in your data (up to 32,000 characters). Q&A automatically moves the cursor from line to line as you type. If you want some information to appear on a new line of its own, press Enter and type it in.

You can move the cursor with the mouse or the arrow keys and type over mistakes. You can also insert information as follows:

1. Position the cursor where you want to add data and press Insert.

2. Q&A displays `Ins` just above the status line.

3. Type in your entries.

4. Press Insert again to return to the field editor's normal state in which you can type over data.

When you've finished entering data with the field editor, press F10. Q&A displays as much of the information you added as the field allows, and ends the display with a right arrow to indicate that you have expanded this field. Whenever you move the cursor to an expanded field and try to edit its data, Q&A prompts you to press F6 as shown in Figure 4-3. You can continue filling out the form and save this record.

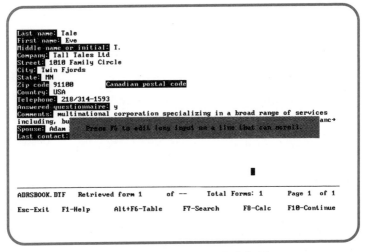

Figure 4-3. A record with expanded field prompt.

Correcting Mistakes After Adding a Record

If you want to correct a record you've added during a session, you can retrieve it by pressing F9. Each time you press F9, Q&A goes back one record added during the session. When you find the one you want, you can make corrections by typing over information. When you've finished your corrections, press F10 to save the revised record.

You can always correct a record you added in an earlier session with the **S - Search/Update** option in the File Menu. See Lesson 6 for details on retrieving records with this option.

A Note about Saving Records

It's important to understand how Q&A saves data with the **A - Add data** option so that you don't lose information or inadvertently overwrite data that you want to keep.

> **Overwriting Data** *Overwrite* means *replacing* data in an existing record with new or altered information; you cannot retrieve overwritten data unless you have a backup copy of the database. See Lesson 8 for details on backing up a database.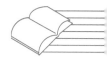

Q&A saves the data in a record each time you get another record by pressing F10 or F9. If you enter data for a new record, Q&A assigns it a record number and adds it to the database. If you make changes to the data in an existing record, Q&A replaces the old data in the record with the altered data. Q&A does not change the record number nor does it retain a copy of previous data in the record.

Q&A does not save data when you press Esc after entering data for a new record or changing data in an existing record. It does, however, display a warning message (like the one shown in Figure 4-4) that requires a confirmation.

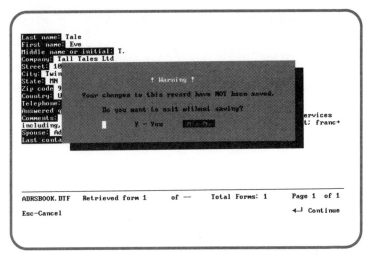

Figure 4-4. A Q&A warning message.

In this lesson, you've learned the basics of adding and editing records in your database. The next lesson provides tips on how to speed up data entry so that you can build your database more efficiently.

Lesson 5

Speeding Up Data Entry with Ditto

In this lesson, you'll learn how to copy duplicate information and optimize your data entry sessions.

The Ditto Feature

When you're entering information in your database, you can use Q&A's Ditto feature to copy information from the record you just added rather than enter it again. This feature can save you a lot of time, especially if much of your data differs only slightly.

Copying Information in Fields

Ditto is only active when you're using the **A - Add data** option from the File Menu and you have a blank data entry form displayed. To duplicate information from the same field in the record you just added, follow these steps:

1. Display a blank data entry form by pressing F10.

2. Position the cursor in your target field.

3. Simultaneously press Shift and F5.

29

Target Field The target field is the field *to which* you're copying data.

If you have a mouse, you can copy the data from the same field as follows:

1. Place the mouse pointer in your target field and click the left mouse button.

2. Put the mouse pointer over **F5-Ditto** in the key assignment line and click the left mouse button, as shown in Figure 5-1.

Cursor   Key Assignment Line

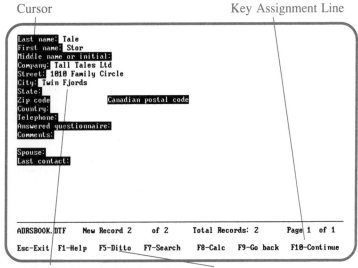

Data Copied from the Previous Record   Mouse Pointer

Figure 5-1. Copying field data with a mouse.

Q&A copies information from the same field in your previous record to the record you're now creating. Ditto is not active when you retrieve your previous record by pressing F9.

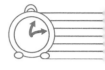

Using Ditto If you have a lot of duplicate information, organize your data entry session so that you can use Ditto to copy data from your previous record.

Copying Information in Entire Records

Just as you can use the Ditto feature to copy information from fields, you can use it to copy the entire contents of the previous record. To duplicate a record:

1. Display a blank data entry form by pressing F10.

2. Simultaneously press Shift and F5.

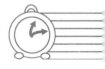

Creating Duplicate Records If most of the data you need to enter differs only slightly, use Ditto to create duplicate records and then go back and edit individual fields.

In this lesson, you've learned how to copy information from individual fields and entire records when you're adding records to your database. The next lesson focuses on how you can quickly retrieve records from your database.

Lesson 6

Retrieving Records from Your Database

In this lesson, you'll learn how to retrieve individual records and define a retrieval specification for calling up groups of records.

The Retrieve Spec Screen

To view or update the information in a database, you need to retrieve the records you've added to it. To locate records, follow these steps:

1. Start Q&A.

2. Select **F - File** from the Main Menu and **S - Search/ Update** from the File Menu.

3. With the cursor in the File Name: box at the bottom of the screen, press the space bar and then press Enter.

4. Select the name of your database from the list of files.

5. Q&A displays the blank form for your database and `Retrieve Spec` on the status line, as shown in Figure 6-1.

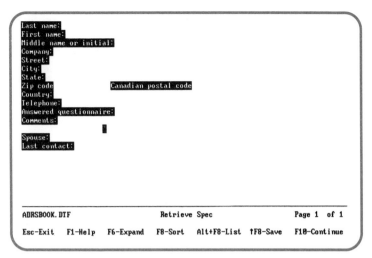

```
Last name:
First name:
Middle name or initial:
Company:
Street:
City:
State:
Zip code          Canadian postal code
Country:
Telephone:
Answered questionnaire:
Comments:

Spouse:
Last contact:




ADRSBOOK.DTF              Retrieve Spec              Page 1  of  1

Esc-Exit   F1-Help   F6-Expand   F8-Sort   Alt+F8-List   ↑F8-Save   F10-Continue
```

Figure 6-1. A sample Retrieve Spec screen.

Retrieving All the Records in a Database

If you want to get all the records in your database, simply press F10 after Q&A displays the Retrieve Spec screen. Q&A shows in form view the first record it locates. Continue to display each of the records in form view by pressing F10. You can also display records in table view by pressing Alt and F6 simultaneously.

Retrieving a Specific Record

Rather than calling up all the records in your database, you can define a *retrieve spec* to locate a single record. For example, to locate and view the record of an individual with a unique last name in your address book database, follow these steps:

    1. Load the Retrieve Spec screen for your database.

33

2. Type in the name in the appropriate field and press F10.

3. Q&A displays that record's data in form view.

 Retrieve Spec A *retrieve spec* is a group of restrictions you enter on the Retrieve Spec screen. Q&A searches all the records in your database and retrieves only those that match the conditions you set.

Retrieving a Group of Records

Once you've created a large database, you won't want to retrieve all records when you're looking only for a particular group. You can find just the ones you want by entering restrictions in the fields on the Retrieve Spec screen. For example, Figure 6-2 shows how you could fill in the Retrieve Spec screen to find all of the records for a particular city in your address book database.

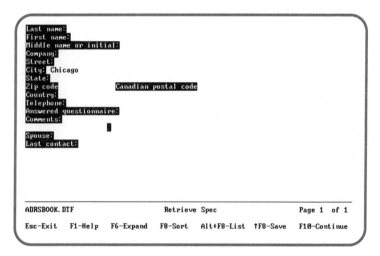

Figure 6-2. A sample retrieve spec to search for `Chicago`.

Saving a Retrieve Spec

You can save time in locating records that you might want to see repeatedly by defining and saving a retrieve spec. After you've filled in the Retrieve Spec form, save it by following these steps:

1. Press Shift and F8 simultaneously.

2. Q&A displays a box (shown in Figure 6-3) in which you can enter a name for the retrieve spec.

3. Type a name such as **AREA CODE 415**.

4. Press Enter.

5. Q&A saves the retrieve spec with the name you entered.

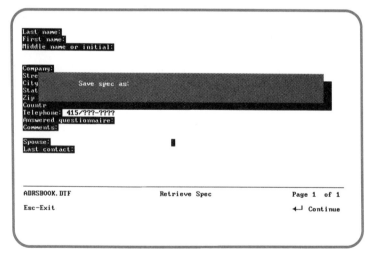

Figure 6-3. A retrieve spec with Save Spec as: box.

You can press F10 to use the retrieve spec now, or you can go on to other work and use it later.

Loading a Saved Retrieve Spec

To load a retrieve spec that has been saved in a database, follow these steps:

1. Select **S - Search/Update** from the File Menu.

2. If your database file name isn't already in the File Name: box at the bottom of the screen, press Enter and select it from the list Q&A displays. Otherwise, just press Enter.

3. When Q&A displays the blank retrieve spec form, press Alt and F8 simultaneously to display a list of retrieve spec names like the one shown in Figure 6-4.

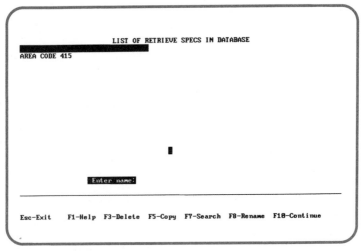

Figure 6-4. A sample list of retrieve spec names.

4. Select the retrieve spec you want and press F10.

5. When Q&A displays your retrieve spec, you can press F10 to get all the records that meet its conditions.

In this lesson, you've learned how to use just a few of Q&A's searching criteria. You can specify restrictions to locate records that exactly match your conditions or match a range of conditions. You can also set up a retrieve spec to look for all records that do *not* match certain criteria. See the Table of Features at the back of this book for a list of some of the sophisticated retrieval capabilities of Q&A. In the next lesson, you learn to sort the data in your Q&A database.

Lesson 7

Sorting Data

In this lesson, you'll learn how to sort records in your database and define and save a sorting specification that you can use over and over.

Sort Level and Sort Order

Although Q&A stores records in the order you added them, you can retrieve them in the order you want by defining a sorting specification. A Q&A *sort spec* is very similar to a retrieve spec (described in Lesson 6). With it you can specify

- Sorting level (the priority you assign to a field)

- Sorting order (the sequence in which you want records arranged)

For example, if you want to sort your address book database first by state and then by city, you should specify a primary sorting level of **1** for the State field and a secondary sorting level of **2** for the City field. Similarly, to arrange the records alphabetically, you should specify **as** (ascending, A to Z) for their respective sorting orders. You can arrange textual records alphabetically (A to Z or Z to A) and numeric data in ascending (low to high) or descending (high to low) order.

Sorting Records

To sort the records you retrieve, follow these steps:

1. Select **F - File** from the Main Menu and **S - Search/ Update** from the File Menu.

2. With the cursor in the File name: box at the bottom of the screen, press the space bar and then press Enter.

3. Select your database from the list of files.

4. When Q&A displays the blank database form with `Retrieve Spec` at the bottom, press F8.

5. Q&A displays the blank form on a Sort Spec screen as illustrated in Figure 7-1.

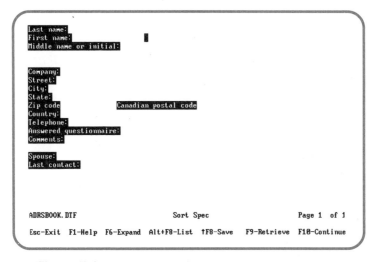

Figure 7-1. A blank Sort Spec screen.

6. Move the cursor to the field to which you want to assign a primary sorting level and type **1** followed by **as** or **ds** for the sorting order.

7. Move the cursor to the field to which you want to assign a secondary sorting level and type **2** followed by **as** or **ds**. You can skip this step if you don't need to sort secondarily.

8. Press F10 to retrieve your records sorted as you specified. Q&A displays the first record in form view.

9. Press Alt and F6 simultaneously to look at the records in table view.

Saving Your Sort Spec

As with retrieve specs, you'll have some sort specs that you'll want to use repeatedly. To name and save a sort spec, follow these steps:

1. After you've filled in the Sort Spec screen, press Shift and F8 simultaneously to save your sort spec. Q&A displays the sort spec with a box superimposed on it as shown in Figure 7-2.

2. With the cursor in the box, type in a name like **ALPHA BY NAME**.

3. Press Enter.

4. To make sure you saved the sort spec with the name you intended, press Alt and F8 simultaneously to display a list of sort specs in your database.

Saving from Table View To save the sort spec from table view, press Esc and repeat steps 1 through 8 in the preceding section.

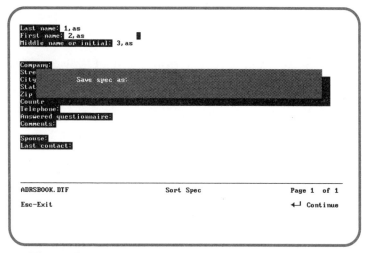

Figure 7-2. Sort Spec with the Save Spec as: box.

Loading a Sort Spec

A powerful feature of Q&A is the ability to use retrieval and sorting specifications you've defined to get groups of records you might want to view or update repeatedly. To retrieve the records from your database with a retrieve spec and sort spec you saved in it:

1. Select S - **Search/Update** from the File Menu.

2. With the cursor in the File name: box at the bottom of the screen, press the space bar and then press Enter.

3. Select your database from the list of files.

4. When Q&A displays the blank retrieve spec form, press Alt and F8 simultaneously to display a list of retrieve specs in your database.

5. Select your retrieve spec and press F10.

41

6. When Q&A displays your retrieve spec, press F8 and then Alt and F8 simultaneously.

7. Select your sort spec from the list Q&A displays. Press F10.

8. Now press F10 to get all the records that meet the criteria of *both* your retrieve and sort specs.

9. Press Alt and F6 simultaneously to display your records in table view.

In this lesson, you've learned how to define and save a sort spec and discovered how to use it with a retrieve spec. These are useful tools for updating information in your database, the topic of the next lesson.

Lesson 8

Updating Your Database

In this lesson, you'll learn how to edit records in your database and duplicate it for safekeeping.

Editing and Deleting Retrieved Records

Just as you must maintain an address book to keep it current, you'll also need to revise information in your database. To update your database, follow these steps:

1. Select **F - File** from the Main Menu and **S - Search/ Update** from the File Menu.

2. With the cursor in the File name: box at the bottom of the screen, press the space bar and then press Enter.

3. Select your database from the list of files.

4. Retrieve and sort the records you want to edit as described in Lessons 6 and 7.

Q&A displays in form view the first record that matches your specifications.

Editing in Form View

In form view, Q&A displays one record at a time. You can edit a record using one or more of these editing procedures:

- Typing over the information you want to change

- Typing new data in empty fields

- Deleting information with Backspace, Delete, or some of the active keys

- Pressing F10 to save the edited record and go on to the next one

- Pressing F9 to save the edited record and get the previous one

- Pressing Shift and F10 simultaneously to save your work and end the session

Before editing a record, press F1 and then Page Down to display both of Q&A's help screens (pictured in Figures 8-1 and 8-2) describing active keys and their functions in form view. Notice that several keys delete information in different ways—by the word, by the line, from the current cursor position, and by the entire record. If you accidentally press one of these keys and don't want to lose the information you deleted, recover it by following these steps:

1. Press Esc.

2. Select Y - Yes from the Warning screen Q&A displays.

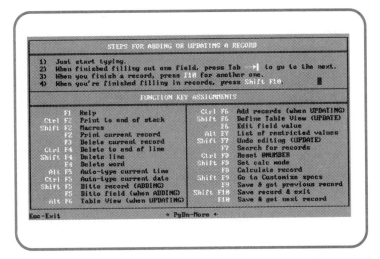

Figure 8-1. Steps for Adding or Updating a Record help screen.

Figure 8-2. Moving Around the Form help screen.

Q&A returns to the File Menu without saving any changes to the record—including your unintentional deletion. You can now start another editing session and continue updating your database.

45

If, after accidentally deleting information, you press F9, F10, or Shift and F10 simultaneously, Q&A saves your altered record. You will have to re-enter any information you inadvertently removed.

Editing in Table View

When you need to modify information in a number of records, you can expedite your work by using table view. To edit data in table view, follow these steps:

1. After Q&A displays the first record that matches your retrieve and sort specs, press Alt and F6 simultaneously.

2. When Q&A displays your records, you can press F1 and then Page Down to display Q&A's help screens describing the active keys and their functions for browsing in table view.

Browsing *Browsing* means looking at records by moving the highlight bar around the table.

3. Press Esc to return to table view.

4. Move the highlight bar to the first field you want to edit and start typing in your changes. Notice that the highlight bar disappears to indicate that you are now editing in table view.

5. To display both of Q&A's help screens describing the keys that are active for editing in table view, press F1 and then Page Down.

6. Press Esc to return to table view and make your changes.

7. Press Shift and F10 simultaneously to save your work and return to the File menu.

Using Backup To Safeguard Your Information

It's prudent to back up your database frequently, and it's especially important to make a backup copy of your database *before* you do any editing. You need to maintain copies of your database so that you can recover from unexpected power failures that might damage your files or errors that you might introduce while working with your data. You should regularly copy your database files onto diskettes and store a set in a safe place away from your workplace.

Backup Copies *Backup* means a duplicate set of your database files.

To use Q&A's backup facility, follow these steps:

1. Select **F - File** from the Main Menu and **U - Utilities** from the File Menu.

2. From the File Utilities Menu, select **B - Backup Database.**

3. With the cursor in the File name: box shown in Figure 8-3, press the space bar and then press Enter.

4. Select your database from the list of files.

5. Q&A displays a box at the bottom of the screen (shown in Figure 8-4), and proposes C : \QA\ (your Q&A directory) as the destination for your backup copies.

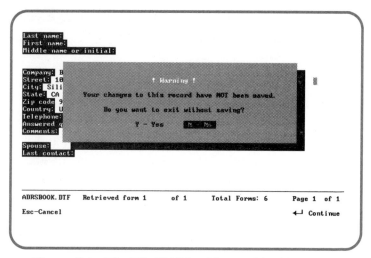

Figure 8-3. The File Utilities Menu with File name: box.

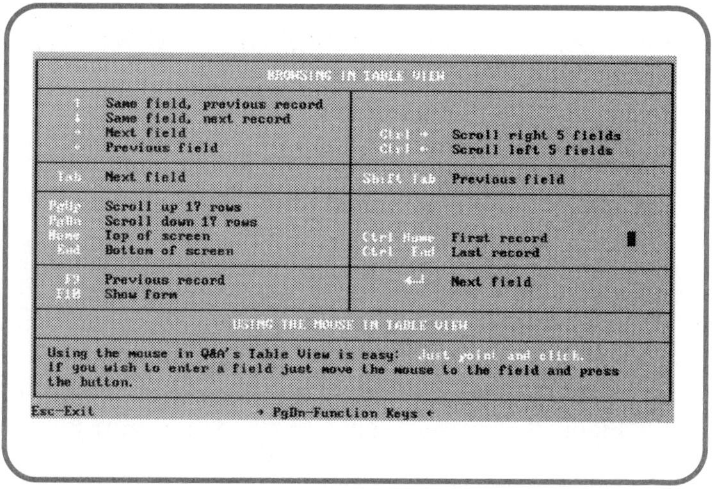

Figure 8-4. The File Utilities Menu with Backup to: box.

6. To back up your database on diskette, press Backspace to remove **C:\QA** and type in the floppy disk drive destination. Then type the name of your database and press Enter. For example, typing **A:\ADRSBOOK** and pressing Enter copies both

the ADRSBOOK.DTF and ADRSBOOK.IDX files comprising an address book database to a diskette in drive A.

7. After copying your files, Q&A displays a confirmation message at the bottom of the screen.

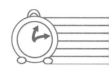

Labeling Disks Don't forget to label your diskette with the database file name and the date. Labeling will help you locate the right version as your archive of backup copies grows.

In this lesson, you've learned how to update and back up a database. The next lesson covers redesigning a database form.

Lesson 9

Changing a Database Form

In this lesson, you'll learn how to redesign and customize your database form.

The Redesign Screen

You can always change a database form with Q&A, but before you do, it's a good idea to back up your database. See "Using Backup To Safeguard Your Information" in Lesson 8. To redesign your database form, follow these steps:

1. Select **F - File** from the Main Menu and **D - Design file** from the File Menu.

2. From the Design Menu, select **R - Redesign a file**. Q&A displays a Data file: box at the bottom of the screen as shown in Figure 9-1.

3. With the cursor in the Data file: box, press the space bar and then press Enter.

4. Select your database from the list of files.

5. Q&A displays your blank database form on a Redesign screen as illustrated in Figure 9-2.

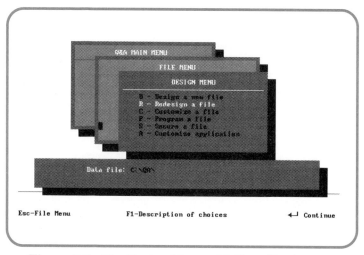

Figure 9-1. The Design Menu with Data file: box.

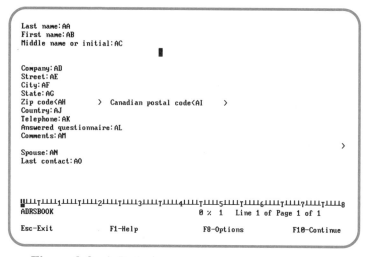

Figure 9-2. A Redesign screen.

Notice that your database form appears as you designed it, but each field begins with a two-character code that Q&A supplied automatically. These internal codes are the mechanism by which Q&A keeps track of the data for each field in each record. To avoid damaging your database, always observe these rules when redesigning a form:

- When you move a field, move the code with it.

- When you delete a field, delete its code.

- When you add a field, let Q&A supply the code automatically when it updates your form design.

- If you accidentally erase a code, retype it precisely as it appeared. If you can't remember it, press Esc. Then select **Y - YES** on the Warning screen pictured in Figure 9-3 to return to the File Menu and start over.

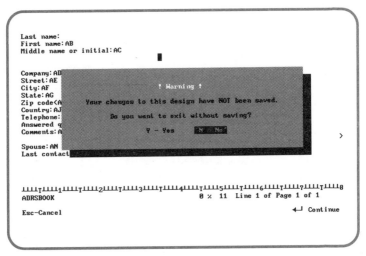

Figure 9-3. The Warning screen.

Editing Your Form Design

The functions described in Lesson 2 for designing a form are also available for redesigning it. In addition, you can always press F1 from the Redesign screen to display a help screen (shown in Figure 9-4) summarizing common editing procedures. When you finish editing your form:

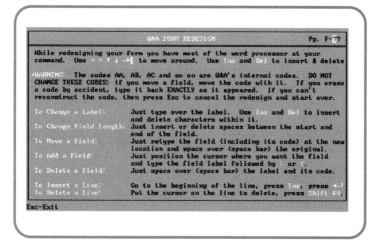

Figure 9-4. Q&A Form Redesign help screen.

1. Press F10 to save your redesigned form and display the format spec.

2. Make any necessary changes to field information types and press F10 to save them.

3. If your form contains date, hour, money, or number fields, Q&A displays the Global Format Options screen.

4. Select the global formatting options you want and press F10 to save them.

5. If you added fields with text or keyword information types to your form and you've already "taught" the Query Guide about your database, Q&A displays the screen (shown in Figure 9-5) providing the opportunity to add these fields to your Query Guide index now. Refer to Lesson 24 for details on teaching the Query Guide.

6. Select Yes - Add fields or No - Don't add fields.

7. Q&A returns to the File Menu.

53

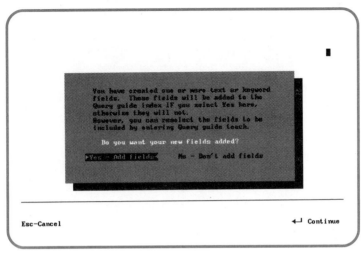

Figure 9-5. Add Fields to Query Guide Index screen.

Losing Data If you delete a field, Q&A displays a warning message advising you that you might lose some data. Press Esc to retain the data and lose your edits; otherwise, press F10 to return to step 1.

Adding Custom Features

Q&A lets you further tailor your database form to speed up data entry and enhance its appearance. The **C - Customize a file** selection in the Design Menu provides the following options:

- **F - Format values** for controlling the information type of data entered in a field and how that data is formatted

- **R - Restrict values** for limiting the range of values you can enter in a field

- **T - Field template** for controlling the format of data entry and automatically supplying commonly used characters

- **I - Set initial values** for automatically filling in fields with common values

- **S - Speed up searches** for accelerating the retrieval of records for fields you frequently use when searching for information

- **D - Define custom help** for preparing special help messages for any field

- **C - Change palette** for selecting colors, shading, and underlining to enhance your form

The following example shows just one way you can customize a field by creating a template that automatically supplies characters and imposes a pattern on the data you enter into it later. This is particularly useful for foreign postal codes and telephone numbers. To create a template for a seven-character text field called Canadian postal code, you would follow these steps:

1. Select D - Design file from the File Menu and C - Customize a file from the Design Menu.

2. Type the name of your database in the Data file: box at the bottom of the screen, and press Enter.

3. Select T - Field template from the Customize Menu.

4. Move the cursor to the Canadian postal code field and type $$$ $$$.

   Each $ stands for any alphanumeric character that you can enter for the two three-character components of a Canadian postal code. The blank in the template separates the two components. Q&A automatically supplies the blank and moves the cursor to the next position to the right when you enter postal code data in the field later.

5. Press F10 to return to the Customize Menu.

6. Press Esc repeatedly to return to the Main Menu and exit Q&A.

Field templates can reduce the amount of time it takes you to enter data in your database. However, you can create templates only for fields with a text information type.

In this lesson, you've learned how to edit your form and how to add a field template to it. The next lesson describes how to print forms and records in your database.

Lesson 10

Printing Forms and Records

In this lesson, you'll learn how to generate quick printouts of your form and records while you're adding records to your database. You'll also learn how to define, save, and use print specs to print data with Q&A.

If you haven't used the **U - Utilities** selection from the Main Menu to specify which printing devices are connected to your computer, refer to "Specifying Printers" at the back of the book before continuing with this lesson.

Quick Print While Adding Data

When you're entering new records in your database with the **A - Add data** selection from the File Menu, printing them is often useful for proofreading or reminding you of what information you've already added during a session. To print the record displayed on your monitor, follow these steps:

1. Press F2 to display the File Print Options screen shown in Figure 10-1.

2. You can change the default options by moving the highlight bar with the arrow keys or the mouse and selecting the one you want. For descriptions of the

57

options, press F1 and then Page Down to display Q&A's help screens.

```
                      FILE PRINT OPTIONS
                      ═══════════════════
 Print to.....:   ▶PtrA◀  PtrB   PtrC   PtrD   PtrE   DISK   SCREEN

 Page preview.................:   Yes  ▶No◀

 Type of paper feed...........:   Manual  ▶Continuous◀  Bin1   Bin2   Bin3

 Print offset.................:   0

 Printer control codes........:

 Print field labels...........:  ▶Yes◀  No

 Number of copies.............:   1

 Number of records per page....:  1

 Number of labels across.......:  ▶1◀  2   3   4   5   6   7   8

 Print expanded fields........:   Yes  ▶No◀
 ─────────────────────────────────────────────────────────────
 ADRSBOOK.DTF           Print Options for current form
 Hewlett Packard LaserJet II/D/P/III (Port) »» LPT1
 Esc-Exit            F1-Help           F8-Define Page          F10-Continue
```

Figure 10-1. The File Print Options screen.

Defaults *Default options* are the ones that are high-lighted when Q&A first displays an options screen.

3. Press F10 to print your current record.

To print only the form:

● Follow steps 1 through 3 at the beginning of your session before you add a new record.

Or

● Press F10 until Q&A displays an empty form and then follow steps 1 through 3.

Printing All Records To print all the records you've added in a session, press F9 repeatedly until you return to the first record, press Ctrl and F2 simultaneously, and then press F10.

Defining and Saving a Print Spec

For printing selected groups of records, lists compiled from data in specified fields, and sets of information on pre-printed forms, you should define and save print specs that you can use again for these tasks you're likely to repeat.

> **Print Spec** A *print spec* is a group of specs that you define with the **P - Print** option from the File Menu and the **D - Design/Redesign a spec** selection from the Print Menu; it determines what data to print, how it's formatted, and the device on which it's printed.

The following are the major steps required to define a print spec:

1. Select F - File from the Main Menu and P - Print from the File Menu.

2. With the cursor in the File name: box at the bottom of the screen, press the space bar and then press Enter.

3. Select the name of your database from the list of files. Q&A displays the Print Menu shown in Figure 10-2.

4. Now select D - Design/Redesign a spec from the Print Menu.

5. After Q&A displays the List of Print Specs in Database screen shown in Figure 10-3, type a name for your print spec in the Enter name: field and press F10 to display a retrieve spec form.

6. Fill in the empty retrieve spec form to specify the records from which you want to print data and press F8 to display a sort spec form.

7. Complete the sort spec form to set the order in which you want your data printed and press F10.

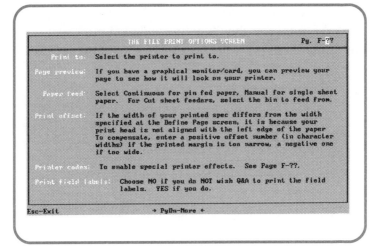

Figure 10-2. The Print Menu.

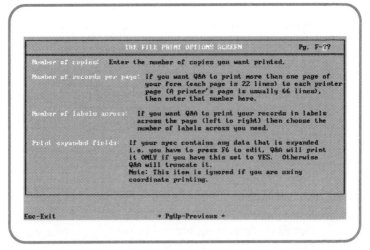

Figure 10-3. The List of Print Specs in Database screen.

8. Q&A displays a fields spec form in which you can specify the fields from which you want to print data and where you want it to appear on the printed page.

(Refer to the next section for information on fields spec entries.) When you've finished typing in fields spec codes, press F10 to display the File Print Options screen.

9. Select the device on which you want to print and any other options appropriate to your system, and press F8 to display the Define Page screen pictured in Figure 10-4.

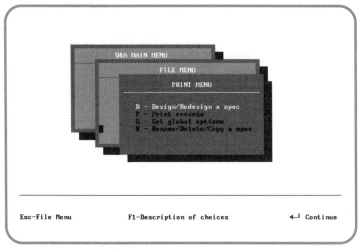

Figure 10-4. The Define Page screen.

10. Define your page size, headers, and footers and press F10 to save your print spec.

11. Q&A displays the confirmation screen shown in Figure 10-5. Select **Y - Yes** to print your data or **N - No** to return to the Print Menu.

You can use your print spec in the future by selecting **P - Print** from the File Menu, **P - Print records** from the Print Menu, and the name of your print spec from the list Q&A displays.

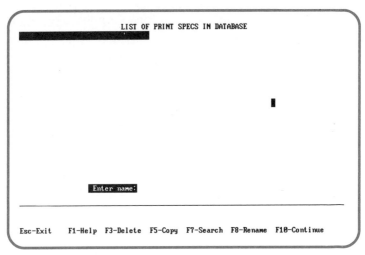

Figure 10-5. The Print confirmation screen.

Printing Entire Records To print all records in their entirety, leave your retrieve and fields specs blank when defining your print spec.

Selecting Fields To Print with the Fields Spec

When you want to print data from only some fields, you must specify them in the fields spec form. For each field from which you want to print information, type

- An X to print the field's data and begin printing data from subsequent fields on the next line

- A + (plus sign) to print the field's data, skip one space, and start printing data from subsequent fields on the same line

For example, the Fields Spec screen shown in Figure 10-6 shows the entries you'd make to print a telephone list from an address book database.

With the fields spec you can also select other sophisticated printing options that are beyond the scope of this book. These include:

- Reordering fields when printing data from them

- Applying text enhancements such as boldface or specific type fonts

- Precisely positioning data on preprinted forms

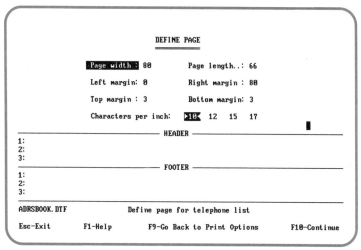

Figure 10-6. Sample Fields Spec entries.

In this lesson, you've learned how to print records while you're adding them to your database and explored how to define and save a print spec for future use. Later lessons describe how to print reports, word processing documents, and mailing labels.

Introduction to Reports

In this lesson, you'll learn to select records and start defining a basic report.

Basic Steps in Creating a Report

Although you can extract and print information from your database as described in Lesson 10, the **R - Report** selection in Q&A's Main Menu lets you produce reports that require more sophisticated data manipulation and formatting. For example, you can set up reporting procedures that not only retrieve data, but also perform calculations and produce complex tables of information.

Reports *Reports* are simply tables of information extracted or derived from your database. You set the contents of the table's rows and columns by specifying criteria in the screens that Q&A displays after you select **R - Report** from the Main Menu.

Whether you're creating a columnar report (see Figure 11-1) or a cross-tabular report (see Figure 11-2), the initial steps for producing them are the same. To begin designing a report:

```
   Last Name        First Name     Department         Position
 ----------------  -------------  -------------  -----------------------
 Abrams            Judy           OPS            Manager
 Billingsgate      Rudy           ADMIN          Admin. Assistant
 Brothers          John           EXEC           President
 Carter            James          SALES          Outside
 Criswell          Ernest         ADMIN          Assistant
 Darwin            Charles        R&D            Engineer
 Dean              Sarah          SALES          Sales Administrator
 Eisenstein        Joseph         LEGAL          Chief Counsel
 Foobah            Dorian         PROMO          Manager                ▌
 Fremont           Sam            SALES          Outside
 Gallway           James          ADMIN          Manager
 Guy               Mary           SALES          Regional Sales Manager
 Gyorfi            Natalia        SALES          Outside
 Jacobson          Will           SALES          Regional Sales Manager
 Jeffers           David          SALES          Outside
 Johnson           Charles        EXEC           Plant Manager
 Johnson           Mildred        ADMIN          Secretary
 Johnson           Nick           SALES          National Sales Manager
 Jones             Jane           SALES          Sales Administrator
 ───────────────────────────────────────────────────────────────────────
 EMPLOYEE.DTF

 Esc-Exit  F2-Reprint   { → ← ↑ ↓ }-Scroll    Shift+F9-Redesign    F10-Continue
```

Figure 11-1. A **Q&A Employee Directory** columnar report.

```
                            Sex
                    ---------------------      Total
 Department         FEMALE        MALE         Salary
 ------------      ----------   ----------   -------------
 ACCNT             $35,000.00        $0.00     $35,000.00
 ADMIN             $47,000.00   $91,000.00    $138,000.00
 EXEC                   $0.00  $177,000.00    $177,000.00
 LEGAL                  $0.00  $125,000.00    $125,000.00
 OPS               $37,000.00        $0.00     $37,000.00
 PROMO             $25,000.00        $0.00     $25,000.00
 R&D                    $0.00  $143,000.00    $143,000.00          ▌
 SALES            $252,000.00  $370,000.00    $622,000.00
 ============     ==========   ==========   =============
 Total Salary    $396,000.00  $906,000.00  $1,302,000.00

 ───────────────────────────────────────────────────────────────────────
 EMPLOYEE.DTF

 Esc-Exit  F2-Reprint   { → ← ↑ ↓ }-Scroll    Shift+F9-Redesign    F10-Continue
```

Figure 11-2. **Q&A Salary by Sex and Depart** cross-tabular report.

1. Select **R - Report** from the Main Menu and **D - Design/Redesign a report** from the Report Menu shown in Figure 11-3.

65

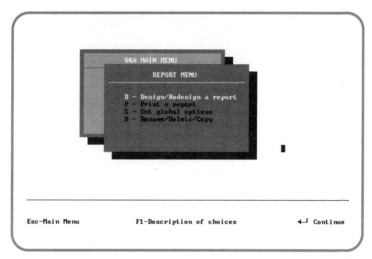

Figure 11-3. The Report Menu.

2. With the cursor in the File name: box at the bottom of the screen, press the space bar and then press Enter.

3. Select the name of your database from the list of files.

4. After Q&A displays a List of Reports in Database screen similar to the one shown in Figure 11-4, type a name for your new report in the Enter name: field and press F10.

5. When Q&A displays the Report Type screen pictured in Figure 11-5, select C - Columnar to design a columnar report (see Lesson 12) or X - Cross tab report to design a cross-tabular report (see Lesson 13).

6. Q&A displays an empty retrieve spec form for your report.

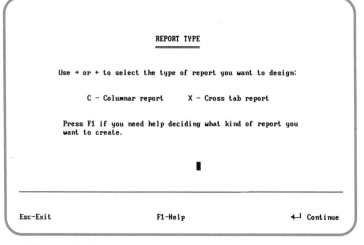

Figure 11-4. A List of Reports in Database screen.

```
                        REPORT TYPE
                        ===========


        Use → or ← to select the type of report you want to design:

             C - Columnar report      X - Cross tab report

          Press F1 if you need help deciding what kind of report you
          want to create.


                              ▮
        _____


Esc-Exit                  F1-Help                    ←┘ Continue
```

Figure 11-5. The Report Type screen.

Selecting Records To Include in Your Report

The retrieve spec determines the individual records from which your report selects and processes data. For either a columnar or cross-tabular report, you can do the following:

- Select data from all records by leaving the retrieve spec blank and pressing F10

- Use a previously defined retrieve spec by simultaneously pressing Alt and F8, selecting the retrieve spec from the list Q&A displays, and pressing F10

- Fill in the blank retrieve spec, simultaneously press Shift and F8, type a name in the Save spec as: box Q&A displays, press Enter to save the retrieve spec, and then press F10

For quick reminders of how to complete a retrieve spec, refer to Lesson 6, "Retrieving Records from Your Database," or press F1 and then Page Down to display Q&A's help screens summarizing retrieval codes.

Using Sample Reports Print Q&A's sample columnar and cross-tabular reports to see if any approximate the type of table you want to produce. If you find one that does, copy it (with F5) and edit its specs to suit your needs.

In this lesson, you've learned how to start defining a report. The steps for defining a columnar report are covered in the next lesson. Lesson 13 outlines the procedure for defining a cross-tabular report.

Lesson 12

Designing a Columnar Report

In this lesson, you'll learn the basics of designing a columnar report.

Description of a Columnar Report

A columnar report shows information from each record matching your retrieve spec, one row at a time. The data for each record appears in columns that you set up by specifying the fields from which you want to extract information. For example, if you want to produce a telephone directory from a database that contains names, addresses, telephone numbers, and other information, you would design a columnar report to display only the data from the name and telephone fields.

Setting up Columns and Rows

After you complete a retrieve spec to select the records that will appear in each row of the report, Q&A displays the database form on a Column/Sort Spec screen as illustrated in Figure 12-1. To specify the fields from which data will be displayed:

69

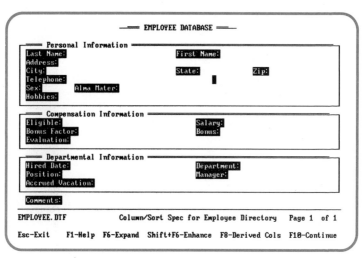

Figure 12-1. Sample Column/Sort Spec screen.

1. Move the cursor to the field containing data for the first column. Type **1**, a comma, and **as** or **ds** (ascending or descending) for its sorting order.

2. Move the cursor to the field containing data for the next column. Type **2**, a comma, and the sorting order you want. Continue until you've specified all the fields containing data to be reported in columns.

3. Press F10 to save the column/sort spec and display the Report Print Options screen. (The Report Print options are described in Lesson 14.)

4. Select print options for your system and press F8.

5. Q&A displays the Define Page screen. Make any changes you want and press F10. (The Define Page screen is described in Lesson 14.)

6. Q&A displays a confirmation screen. Select **Y - Yes** to print your report as it's currently defined or **N - No** to return to the Report Menu.

Defining and Saving a Simple Columnar Report

The following example steps through the basics of defining a simple columnar report that generates a telephone list from all the records in an address book database:

1. With the cursor in the File name: box at the bottom of the Report Menu screen, press the space bar and then press Enter, and select the name of the database. In the example, the database name is **ADRSBOOK.DTF**.

2. In the Enter name: field, type in a report name and press F10. The report name in the example is Phone List.

3. Select C - Columnar report from the Report Type screen.

4. Leave the Retrieve Spec screen blank and press F10 to display the Column/Sort Spec screen.

5. To make an alphabetical telephone list in which last names display first, type 1,as in the Last name: field, 2,as in the First name: field, 3,as in the Middle name or initial: field, and 4 in the Telephone: field as shown in Figure 12-2.

6. Press F10 to display the Report Print Options screen. Select the options appropriate to your system and press F10. (This bypasses the Define Page screen.)

7. Print the report by selecting Y - Yes from the confirmation screen Q&A displays.

The printed report of the sample phone list is shown in Figure 12-3.

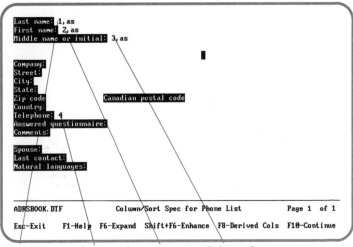

Figure 12-2. Sample entries in a Column/Sort Spec form.

Last name	First name	Middle name or initial	Telephone
History	Liddle		218/314-1593
Martin	Joseph	▮	312/946-8866
Patrick	Henry		415/327-7100
Peters	Thor		218/314-1593
Russell	C.	J.	415/991-9001
Saga	Stor		218/314-6240
Tale	Eve	T.	218/314-1593

ADRSBOOK.DTF
**************************** END OF REPORT *******************************
Esc-Exit   F2-Reprint   { → ← ↑ ↓ }-Scroll   Shift+F9-Redesign   F10-Continue

Figure 12-3. Sample telephone list report.

    In this lesson, you've learned how to create the basic design for a columnar report. The next lesson describes designing a cross-tabular report. Lesson 14 covers formatting and printing reports.

Lesson 13

Designing a Cross-Tabular Report

In this lesson, you'll learn the basics of designing a cross-tabular report. This lesson briefly outlines the process of printing a report; this is covered in Lesson 14.

Like a columnar report, a *cross-tabular report* is a table that shows information from records matching the criteria of your retrieve spec. However, a cross-tabular report extracts data from three fields you specify: the row field, the column field, and the summary field. Cross-tabular reports are appropriate for comparing and summarizing three different types of information stored in your database. For example, the cross-tabular report in Figure 13-1 summarizes data by department, sex, and salary.

Setting up Columns and Rows

After you complete the retrieve spec that determines the records from which data is extracted for your cross-tabular report, Q&A displays the database form on a Cross Tab Spec screen as shown in Figure 13-2. To specify rows and columns:

Row field   Column Field   Summary Field

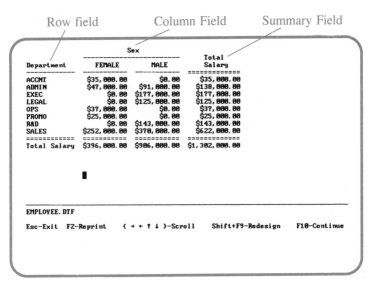

Figure 13-1. Sample cross-tabular report.

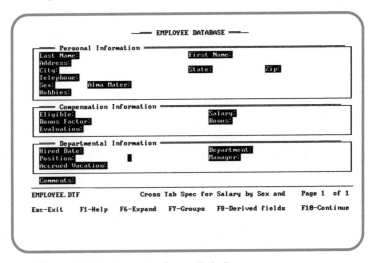

Figure 13-2. Sample Cross Tab Spec screen.

1. Type **row** in the field from which you want to extract data to appear in rows.

2. Type **col** in the field from which you want to extract data to display in columns.

74

3. Type sum in the field from which you want to extract summary data.

4. Press F10 to save your cross tab spec and display the Cross Tab Print Options screen. Make any changes appropriate to your system. (These options are described in Lesson 14.)

5. Press F8 to display the Define Page screen. Make any changes you want and press F10. (The Define Page screen is explained in Lesson 14.)

6. Q&A displays a confirmation screen. Select Y - Yes to print your report as it's currently defined, or N - No to return to the Report menu.

Defining and Saving a Simple Cross-Tabular Report

The following example explains the basics of defining a simple cross-tabular report that tallies the responses to a questionnaire sent to individuals in an address book database:

1. With the cursor in the File name: box at the bottom of the Report Menu screen, press the space bar and then press Enter. Select the name of the database. In the example, the database name is ADRSBOOK.DTF.

2. In the Enter name: field, type in a report name and press F10. The report name in the example is CT-92 Questionnaire Responses.

3. Select X - Cross tab report from the Report Type screen.

4. Leave the Retrieve Spec screen that Q&A displays blank and press F10 to display the Cross Tab Spec screen.

5. To make a report that tallies responses to a questionnaire by state, type **row,c** in the Answered questionnaire: field. The **c** is a calculation code that counts the number of yes and no values in a field. Then type **col, summary** in the State: field as shown in Figure 13-3. In the example, the State: field is both the column field and the summary field. That is, the summary field doesn't have to be a third separate field.

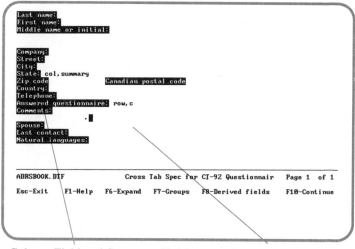

Column Field and Summary Field   Calculation Code

Figure 13-3. Sample entries in a Cross Tab Spec form.

6. Press F10 to display the Cross Tab Print Options screen. Select the options appropriate to your system and press F10. (This bypasses the Define Page screen.)

7. Print your report by selecting **Y - Yes** from the confirmation screen Q&A displays.

The report of the sample response list is shown in Figure 13-4.

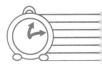

Naming Reports Try to develop a naming protocol that incorporates both the report type and report contents. In the previous example, CT stands for "cross-tabular." A report name can contain 30 or fewer alphanumeric characters.

```
                              State
                         ---------------
Answered questionnaire   CA  IL  MN   Count
------------------------ --  --  --   =====
 n                        0   0   2       2
 y                        2   1   2       5
======================== ==  ==  ==   =====
Count                     2   1   4       7




          ▮

_____

ADRSBOOK.DTF

 Esc-Exit  F2-Reprint   { → ← ↑ ↓ }-Scroll   Shift+F9-Redesign   F10-Continue
```

Figure 13-4. Sample cross-tabular response report.

In this lesson, you've learned how to create the basic design for a simple cross-tabular report. See the "Table of Features" for some of the powerful options Q&A provides for designing very sophisticated reports. Formatting and printing reports are covered in the next lesson.

Formatting and Printing a Report

In this lesson, you'll learn the basic steps for setting up formatting and printing codes for report procedures that you can retrieve for future use.

Formatting a Report

Unless you specify formatting codes in your report's column/sort or cross tab spec, Q&A composes the report following the codes in your database's format spec. To override those codes and customize the appearance of a report that you intend to use again:

1. Select **R - Report** from the Main Menu and **D - Design/Redesign a report** from the Report Menu.

2. With the cursor in the File name: box at the bottom of the screen, press the space bar and then press Enter.

3. Select the name of your database from the list of files.

4. When Q&A displays the List of Reports in Database screen, select the name of your report and press F10.

5. After Q&A displays the Retrieve Spec screen, press F10.

6. On the Column/Sort Spec or Cross Tab Spec screen, move the cursor to the field that you want to format, and place the cursor in the first empty position to the right of the row, column, sorting, and calculation codes.

7. Type your formatting specifications. (See the next section for more information on formatting codes.)

8. Press F10 to save your formatting specifications and display the Print Options screen for your columnar or cross-tabular report.

Formatting Codes

Follow this pattern when typing your formatting specifications:

,f(*code,code,code***)**

Type a comma to separate the row, column, sorting, and calculation codes from your formatting codes. (See Table 14-1 for a summary of formatting codes.) Then type an **f** to specify that what follows are formatting codes. Substitute a formatting code for ***code***, separate the formatting codes with commas, and enclose the formatting codes in parentheses. Press F6 to display the field editor window if your list of formatting codes exceeds the defined field width.

Getting Help For a quick reference to date and time format numbers and the formats they represent, press F1 and then press Page Down repeatedly to display Q&A's formatting help screens.

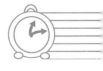

Table 14-1. Report Formatting Codes.

Code	Function
C	Insert commas between numerals
D*n*	Display as a date in format *n* (**1-20**)
H*n*	Display as time in format *n* (**1-3**)
JC	Center
JL	Left justify
JR	Right justify
M	Format as money
N*n*	Display *n* (**1-7**) decimal digits
T	Format as text
U	Set in uppercase characters
WC	Format without commas

Printing a Report

After you've set up formatting codes for your report, you can further tailor its appearance by making selections from the Report Print Options screen (for columnar reports) or the Cross Tab Print Options screen (for cross-tabular reports). Examples of each are shown in Figures 14-1 and 14-2, respectively.

To control precisely the printing of your report, follow these steps:

1. Select the print options appropriate to your system and your report and press F8. Printing options for reports are summarized in Table 14-2.

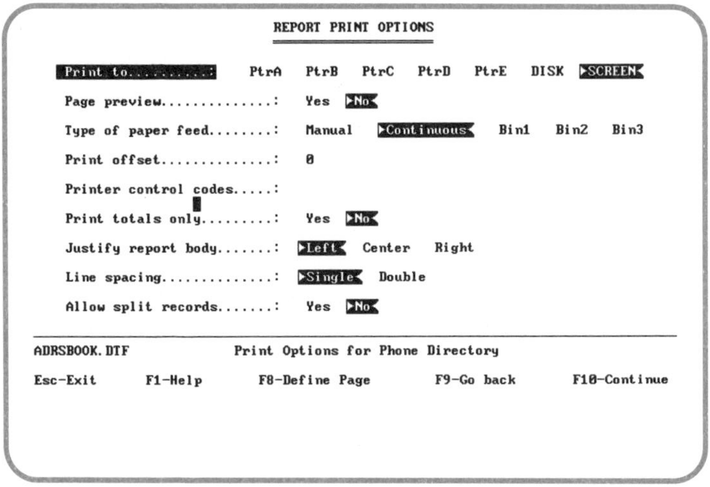

```
                           REPORT PRINT OPTIONS


 ▌Print to...........:  PtrA   PtrB   PtrC   PtrD   PtrE   DISK  ►SCREEN◄

 Page preview.............:   Yes  ►No◄

 Type of paper feed........:   Manual  ►Continuous◄   Bin1   Bin2   Bin3

 Print offset.............:   0

 Printer control codes.....:
                   ▌
 Print totals only.........:   Yes  ►No◄

 Justify report body.......:  ►Left◄  Center   Right

 Line spacing.............:  ►Single◄  Double

 Allow split records.......:   Yes  ►No◄

ADRSBOOK.DTF            Print Options for Phone Directory

Esc-Exit     F1-Help      F8-Define Page      F9-Go back      F10-Continue
```

Figure 14-1. Report Print Options screen.

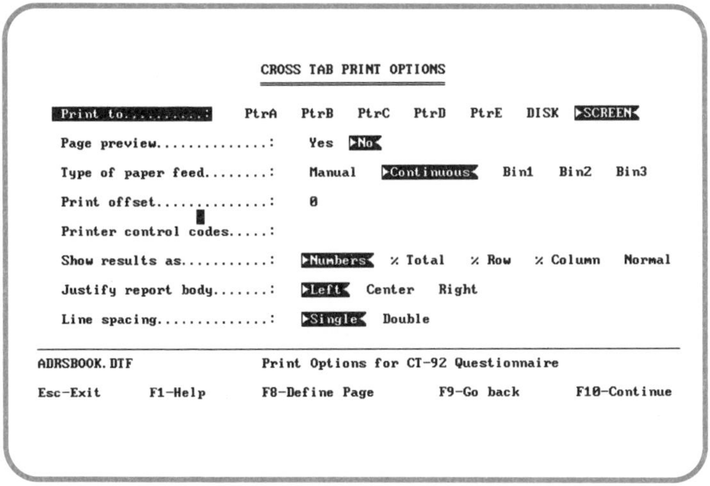

```
                           CROSS TAB PRINT OPTIONS


 ▌Print to...........:  PtrA   PtrB   PtrC   PtrD   PtrE   DISK  ►SCREEN◄

 Page preview.............:   Yes  ►No◄

 Type of paper feed........:   Manual  ►Continuous◄   Bin1   Bin2   Bin3

 Print offset.............:   0
                   ▌
 Printer control codes.....:

 Show results as..........:  ►Numbers◄  % Total   % Row   % Column   Normal

 Justify report body.......:  ►Left◄  Center   Right

 Line spacing.............:  ►Single◄  Double

ADRSBOOK.DTF            Print Options for CT-92 Questionnaire

Esc-Exit     F1-Help      F8-Define Page      F9-Go back      F10-Continue
```

Figure 14-2. Cross Tab Print Options screen.

2. Specify page dimensions, margins, characters per inch, headers, and footers on the Define Page screen that Q&A displays. To set margins:

   • Type a number to specify the number of lines from the top or bottom of the page for the top or bottom margin. For left and right margins, type the number of *character spaces* from the left edge of the page.

Or

● Type a decimal number followed by an " (inch symbol) or c (centimeter) to specify inches or centimeters measured from the nearest edge of the page for all margins and page dimensions.

3. Press F10 to save all of the specifications that define your report.

4. When Q&A displays the confirmation screen shown in Figure 14-3, select Y - Yes to print your report or N - No to return to the Report Menu.

Table 14-2. Report Print Options.

Option	Function
Print to	Specifies printer
Page preview	Displays report on graphics monitor
Paper feed	Specifies paper type and sheet feeder
Print offset	Specifies number of character spaces from left edge of paper at which to start printing
Printer control codes	Specify codes that activate special effects on certain printers
Print totals only	For columnar reports, provides option of printing only totals and subtotals

Table 14-2. (continued)

Option	Function
Show results as	For cross-tabular reports, provides options for printing values as numerals, percentages, or amounts above or below the average
Justify report body	Specifies report's alignment
Line spacing	Specifies single- or double-line spacing
Allow split records	For columnar reports, provides option for forcing data from one record to print on same page

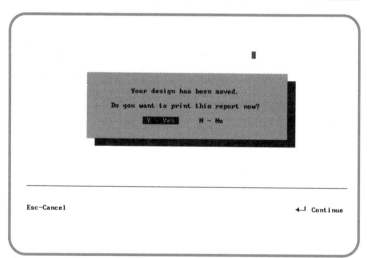

Figure 14-3. Confirmation screen.

You can always load a report procedure that you've named and saved, and print an up-to-date report of the information in your database by:

- Selecting **R - Report** from the Main Menu and **P - Print a report** from the Report Menu

- Pressing the space bar and Enter in the File name: box at the bottom of the screen, and then selecting the name of your database

- Selecting the name of your report from the List of Reports in Database screen

- Selecting **N - No** from the confirmation screen shown in Figure 14-4

You can also redesign report procedures by selecting **D - Design/Redesign a report** from the Report Menu.

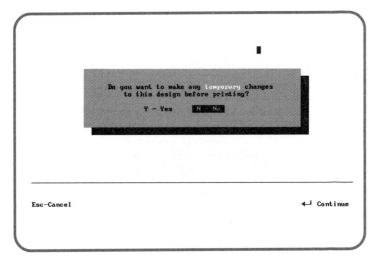

Figure 14-4. Confirmation screen for temporary changes.

In this lesson, you've learned the basic steps for specifying formatting and printing codes for reports that you can save and retrieve to generate up-to-date printouts of information in your database. The next lesson introduces you to Q&A's word-processing facility.

Lesson 15

Introducing Q&A Write

In this lesson, you'll learn to manage document files and use Q&A's word processor to write and save a brief document.

Making a Subdirectory for Documents

You can use Q&A to save and retrieve document files more effectively by setting up a global option to store them in a Q&A subdirectory, as follows:

1. Use the DOS MD (Make Directory) command to create a subdirectory for Q&A documents. For example, at the DOS C:\> prompt, type **md c:\qa\qadocs** and press Enter to make a **qadocs** subdirectory in a **qa** directory on the C drive. (For more information on DOS commands, refer to the "DOS Primer" at the back of this book.)

2. Start Q&A following the instructions in Lesson 2.

3. Select **U - Utilities** from the Main Menu and **S - Set global options** from the Utilities Menu. Q&A displays the Set Global Options screen shown in Figure 15-1.

4. With the cursor in the first position to the right of the path that Q&A displays for the **Q&A Document Files:** option, type the name of your document subdirectory and press F10. The subdirectory name in the example is **qadocs**. Q&A saves your global option setting and returns to the Utilities Menu.

5. Press Esc to return to the Main Menu.

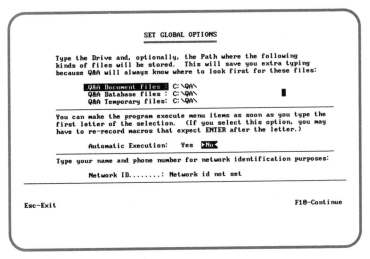

```
                        SET GLOBAL OPTIONS

    Type the Drive and, optionally, the Path where the following
    kinds of files will be stored.  This will save you extra typing
    because Q&A will always know where to look first for these files:

          Q&A Document files : C:\QA\
          Q&A Database files : C:\QA\                          ▮
          Q&A Temporary files: C:\QA\

    You can make the program execute menu items as soon as you type the
    first letter of the selection.  (If you select this option, you may
    have to re-record macros that expect ENTER after the letter.)

          Automatic Execution:   Yes   ▶No◀

    Type your name and phone number for network identification purposes:

          Network ID........: Network id not set


 Esc-Exit                                            F10-Continue
```

Figure 15-1. Set Global Options screen.

Starting Q&A Write

Before you can write or edit a document, you must start Q&A's word processor, as follows:

1. Select **W - Write** from the Main Menu to display the Write Menu shown in Figure 15-2.

2. From the Write Menu select **T - Type/Edit**. Q&A displays the blank Type/Edit screen shown in Figure 15-3.

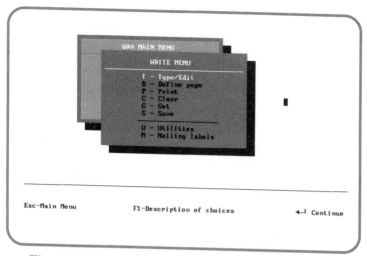

Figure 15-2. Write Menu.

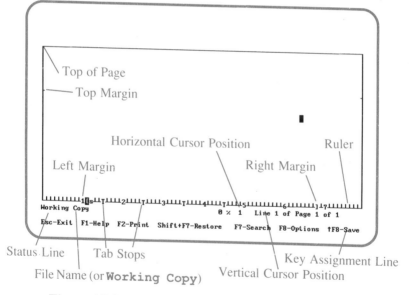

Figure 15-3. Blank Type/Edit screen.

The Type/Edit Screen

When the empty Type/Edit screen appears, you can start typing the contents of a new document. As you type, a bright rectangle moves across the ruler at the bottom of the screen showing the current horizontal cursor position. Beneath the ruler, Write displays a line number indicating the cursor's current vertical position.

Writing a Brief Letter

To draft a short letter like the one shown in Figure 15-4:

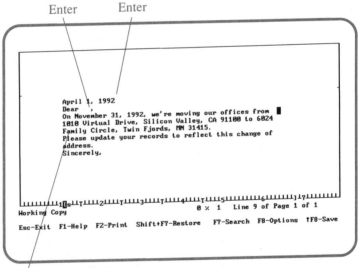

Figure 15-4. Sample letter.

1. With the blank Type/Edit screen displayed, type the date and press Enter.

2. Type the salutation and press Enter.

3. Now type the entire contents of a paragraph and press Enter. Notice that when you run out of room

on a line, Write automatically puts the next word on a new line.

4. Type another paragraph and end it by pressing Enter.

5. Type your closing and press Enter.

Saving Your Document

As a matter of practice, it's prudent to save a document right after you start drafting it, and to continue saving it frequently while you're working on it. Otherwise, if you suffer an unexpected loss of power, you won't be able to recover any of the work you did on the document since you last saved it.

To save a document:

● Simultaneously press Shift and F8.

● When Write displays the Save as: box shown in Figure 15-5, type a name (containing no more than eight alphanumeric characters) for your new document file and press Enter.

Naming Files To remind yourself of what a document file contains, when naming and saving it, type a period and three characters like **ltr** (for *letter*) or **mem** (for *memo*).

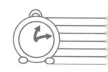

● To save a document file after you've named it, simultaneously press Shift and F8, and then press Enter.

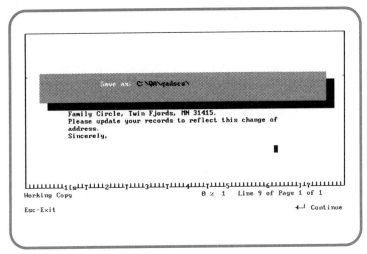

Figure 15-5. Save as: box.

Moving Around a Document

With Write, you can move the cursor by moving the mouse pointer to a new position on the monitor and clicking the left mouse button or by using the cursor keys on the keyboard. Table 15-1 summarizes the keys to press to move the cursor or view different portions of a document.

Table 15-1. Keys for Moving around a Document.

Key	Action
↑Arrow	Moves cursor up one line
↓ Arrow	Moves cursor down one line
← Arrow	Moves cursor left one position
→ Arrow	Moves cursor right one position
Page Down	Displays next screen
Page Up	Displays previous screen
Ctrl End	Moves to end of document
Ctrl Home	Moves to beginning of document

You can also move to a different location with Write's search function (described in Lesson 20.)

Exiting Write

To end a session with the word processor:

1. Press Shift and F8 simultaneously to save the last version of your document.

2. Press Esc to return to the Write Menu.

Exiting Without Saving If you try to end a session without saving the last version of your document, Q&A displays a warning message and gives you an opportunity to save your work.

In this lesson, you've learned how to start Write and use it to create and save a document. The next lesson covers retrieving and editing a document with Write.

Lesson 16

Retrieving, Editing, and Backing Up a Document

In this lesson, you'll learn how to retrieve, edit, and back up a document.

Getting a Document

There are two ways to retrieve a Q&A document:

- From the Write Menu

- From Write's Type/Edit screen

Follow these steps to get a document from the Write Menu:

1. Select **W - Write** from the Main Menu and **G - Get** from the Write Menu.

2. With the cursor in the Document: box that Q&A displays at the bottom of the screen, press the space bar and then press Enter.

3. Select the name of your document file from the List of Files screen (similar to the one shown in Figure 16-1).

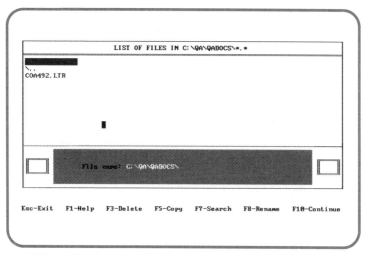

Figure 16-1. List of Files screen.

4. Write retrieves your document and displays it on the Type/Edit screen.

You can retrieve a document from Write's Type/Edit screen as follows:

1. Press F8 to display the Options Menu.

2. Select **D - Documents** and press → to move the highlight to the submenu (shown in Figure 16-2) displayed to the right of the Options Menu.

3. Select the name of your document if it's on the list. Otherwise, select **G - Get a document**. With the cursor in the Document: box, press the space bar and Enter, and then select the name of your document from the list Write displays.

4. Write gets your file and shows its contents on the Type/Edit screen.

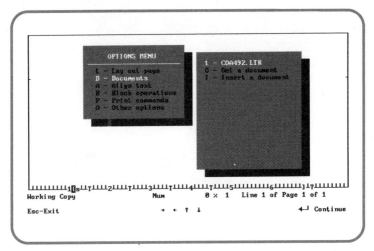

Figure 16-2. Options submenu.

Overwrite and Insert Modes

When you first display the Type/Edit screen and start writing a document or retrieve a previously saved document and start editing it, Write is in overwrite mode. In overwrite mode:

- The cursor is a blinking underscore character.

- Whatever you type *replaces* any old text at the cursor position.

You can add new text without replacing existing copy by pressing Insert to switch to insert mode. In insert mode:

- The cursor is a small square and `Ins` appears on the status line.

- Whatever you type is *added* to the document.

- The new text you insert moves old text to the right of it further right; when you insert enough new copy to push text beyond the right margin, Write automatically moves the text to the next line.

94

To return to overwrite mode:

1. Press Insert.

2. The cursor changes to a blinking underscore and `Ins` disappears from the status line.

Deleting Text

Although Write lets you delete text from a document in a number of ways, the two most useful are

- By character

- By block

To delete text by character,

- Move the cursor to the character you want to remove and press Delete.

  Or

- Press Backspace to delete the character immediately to the left of the cursor.

To delete text by block,

1. Move the cursor to the first character you want to remove and press F3.

2. Press the arrow keys to highlight all the text you want to select for deletion.

3. Press F10 to delete all of the text you highlighted.

You can restore text you deleted as a block by moving the cursor to the position at which you want to insert deleted text and pressing Shift and F7 simultaneously.

Backing Up a Document

Just as it's wise to save a document frequently while you're writing it, you should also make regular backup copies of it. Making a backup copy so that you can recover from unintentional changes is particularly important when you plan to do substantial editing. To back up a document file:

1. From the Write Menu, select U - Utilities and then D - DOS facilities from the Write Utilities Menu shown in Figure 16-3.

2. From the DOS Facilities Menu, select C - Copy a document.

3. With the cursor in the Copy from: box, press the space bar and Enter.

4. Select your document from the list of files.

5. Q&A displays a box at the bottom of the screen (pictured in Figure 16-4), and proposes C:\QA\QADOCS\ (your Q&A document file subdirectory) as the destination for your backup copy.

6. To back up your document file on diskette, press Backspace to remove C:\QA\QADOCS\ and type in the floppy disk drive destination. Then type the name of your document file and press Enter. For example, typing a:\coa492.ltr and pressing Enter, copies a COA492.LTR document file to a diskette in drive A.

7. After copying your file, Q&A displays a confirmation message at the bottom of the screen.

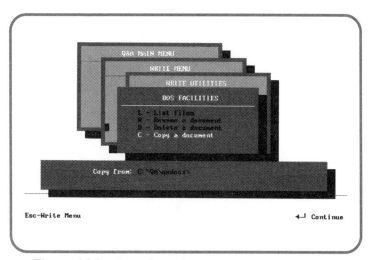

Figure 16-3. Copy from: box.

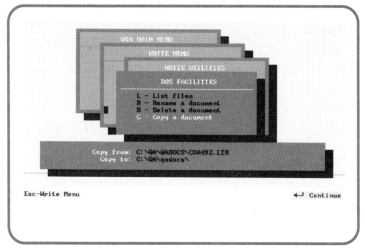

Figure 16-4. Copy to: box.

In this lesson, you've learned how to retrieve, edit, and back up documents. The next lesson covers basic document formatting techniques.

Lesson 17

Basic Document Formatting

In this lesson, you'll learn how to set margins, align single lines of text, indent paragraphs, and set up tabs for your document.

Planning Your Document's Format

You can make the most of Write's document formatting capabilities and save some time if you plan the basic layout of a document before you start writing it. Consider margin sizes, title and heading alignments, indenting entire paragraphs, and tabs for tables. The following sections describe Write's formatting options for these basic conventions.

Setting Margins

To specify your document's page size and the margins that define its print area:

1. Select **W - Write** from the Main Menu and **D - Define page** from the Write Menu. Alternatively, you can select **T - Type/Edit** from the Write Menu, and then press Ctrl and F6 simultaneously.

2. When the Define Page screen (shown in Figure 17-1) is displayed, move the highlight to the setting you want to change.

3. Type a number to specify the number of lines from the top or bottom of the page for the top or bottom margin. For left *and* right margins, type the number of *character spaces* from the left edge of the page.

   Or

   Type a decimal number followed by an " (inch symbol) or c (centimeter) to specify inches or centimeters measured from the nearest edge of the page for all margins and page dimensions.

4. Press F10 to save your new settings for the document you're about to create.

5. Q&A displays a blank Type/Edit screen.

Your margin settings are in effect, and you can start writing your document. You can change these settings later, if you wish.

Aligning Text

For section headings or titles, you can align text with the left or right margin or center it between both margins. While you're writing or editing a document, follow these steps to align text:

1. On the Type/Edit screen, position the cursor anywhere in the line of text you want to align.

2. Press F8.

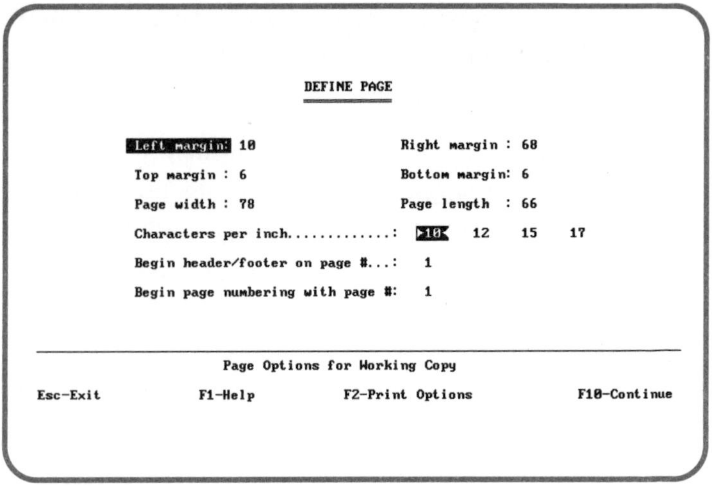

```
                        DEFINE PAGE


        Left margin: 10           Right margin : 68

        Top margin : 6            Bottom margin: 6

        Page width : 78           Page length  : 66

        Characters per inch............:  >10<  12   15   17

        Begin header/footer on page #...:  1

        Begin page numbering with page #:  1



                  Page Options for Working Copy
   Esc-Exit        F1-Help        F2-Print Options        F10-Continue
```

Figure 17-1. Define Page screen.

3. When the Options Menu appears, move the highlight over **A - Align text**.

4. The submenu (shown in Figure 17-2) appears automatically.

5. Press ➡ to move the highlight to the submenu and select **L - Left, C - Center**, or **R - Right**.

6. The Type/Edit screen displays your line of text according to your specification.

To return a line that you centered or aligned with the right margin to its normal state, repeat steps 1 through 4 and select **L - Left** from the Options submenu.

Indenting Text

You can indent entire paragraphs of text for citing quotations, setting up numbered lists, and creating hanging indents by specifying temporary left and right margins while you're writing a document. To indent a paragraph:

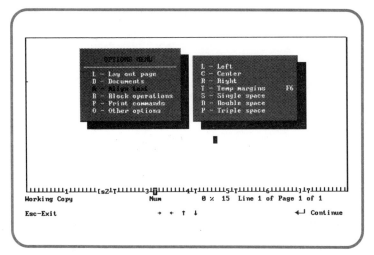

Figure 17-2. Options submenu.

1. From the Type/Edit screen, end the paragraph on which you're working by pressing Enter.

2. Move the cursor to the point where you want the temporary left margin to start.

3. Press F6.

4. Write displays the Set temporary margin: box at the bottom of the screen as shown in Figure 17-3.

5. Select L-Left and Write displays a > (right angle bar) on the ruler to mark the temporary left margin.

6. Now move the cursor to the character position for the temporary right margin and press F6.

7. Select R-Right when the Set temporary margin: box appears. Write displays a < (left angle bar) to mark the temporary right margin.

8. After the cursor returns to the left margin, move it to the tempporary left margin and start typing the contents of the indented paragraph.

101

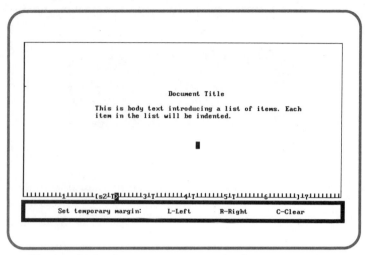

Figure 17-3. Set temporary margin: box.

Temporary margins remain in effect while you're typing until you explicitly clear them by

- Pressing Enter to end the indented paragraph

  Or

- Pressing F6 and selecting **C-Clear** in the Set temporary margin: box.

If you want to remove the temporary margins from an indented paragraph:

- Place the cursor anywhere in it.

- Press F6 and select **C-Clear** in the Set temporary margin: box.

Setting Tabs

You can set tab stops for creating tables and charts in a document as follows:

1. From the Type/Edit screen, press F8 to display the Options Menu and its submenu.

2. Press → to move the highlight to the submenu and select **S - Set tabs**.

3. The cursor moves to the ruler at the bottom of the screen as shown in Figure 17-4.

4. You can now position the cursor where you want a tab stop and type **T** for a regular *left-aligned tab stop* or **D** for a *decimal-aligned tab stop*. To remove an existing tab stop, move the cursor over the **T** and press the space bar or the Delete key.

5. Press F10 to save your settings.

Decimal-Aligned Tabs Decimal-aligned tab stops are appropriate for numeric tables in which you want all the decimal points to line up.

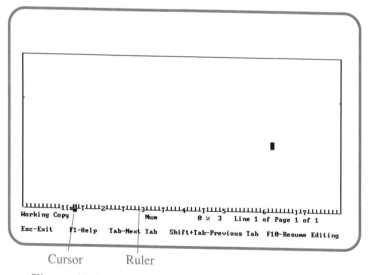

Cursor   Ruler

Figure 17-4. Type/Edit screen for setting tabs.

To move to the next tab stop in your document, press the Tab key. Write inserts the number of spaces between the current cursor position and the next tab stop into your text.

In this lesson you've learned how to set a document's margins, align lines of text, indent paragraphs, and set up tabs. The next lesson describes one of Write's time-saving features, working with blocks of text.

Lesson 18

Working with Blocks of Text

In this lesson, you'll learn the basics of quickly manipulating blocks of text; how to copy them and how to move them.

Block Operations from the Options Menu

Although Write provides a number of ways to manipulate a block of text, the easiest and most comprehensive are available with the **B - Block operations** selection from the Options Menu. To perform a function such as copying or moving a block of text, follow these basic steps:

> **Block** A *block* of text is any group of contiguous characters that you select by highlighting them.

1. On the Type/Edit screen, move the cursor to the first character you want to select and press F8 to display the Options Menu.

2. Select **B - Block operations** to display the Block Operations submenu shown in Figure 18-1.

3. Press ➡ to move the highlight to the submenu and select the block operation you want.

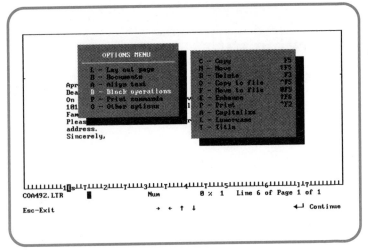

Figure 18-1. Block operations submenu.

Complete the steps required by the block operation you selected. These steps are outlined in the sections that follow.

Copying a Block of Text

To make a copy of a block of text and insert it elsewhere in a document:

1. From the Block operations submenu, select C - Copy.

2. Write displays your document on the Type/Edit screen as illustrated in Figure 18-2.

3. Press the arrow keys to highlight the rest of the text block you want to copy and then press F10.

4. After Write displays your document on the Type/ Edit screen as shown in Figure 18-3, move the cursor to the point at which you want the first character of the copied text block to appear and press F10.

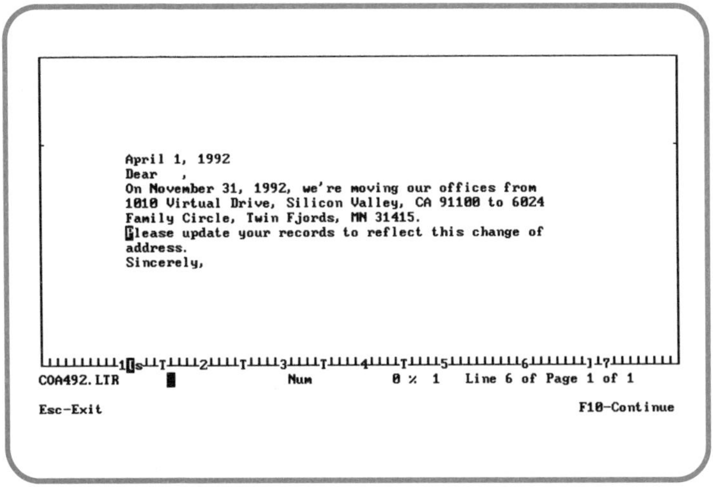

```
                 April 1, 1992
                 Dear   ,
                 On November 31, 1992, we're moving our offices from
                 1010 Virtual Drive, Silicon Valley, CA 91100 to 6024
                 Family Circle, Twin Fjords, MN 31415.
                 ▊lease update your records to reflect this change of
                 address.
                 Sincerely,



  ⊔⊔⊔⊔⊔⊔⊔⊔1▊s⊔⊔T⊔⊔⊔2⊔⊔⊔T⊔⊔⊔3⊔⊔⊔T⊔⊔⊔4⊔⊔⊔T⊔⊔⊔5⊔⊔⊔⊔⊔⊔6⊔⊔⊔⊔⊔7⊔⊔⊔⊔⊔⊔
  COA492.LTR      ▊                  Num        0 % 1  Line 6 of Page 1 of 1

  Esc-Exit                                              F10-Continue
```

Figure 18-2. Type/Edit screen for selecting text block to copy.

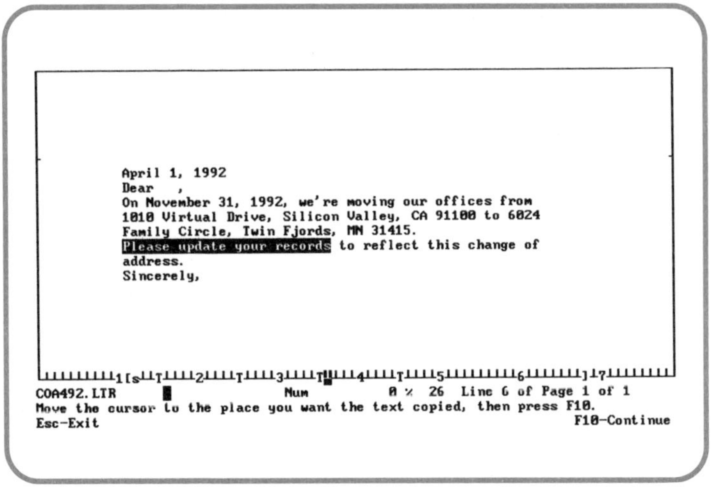

```
                 April 1, 1992
                 Dear   ,
                 On November 31, 1992, we're moving our offices from
                 1010 Virtual Drive, Silicon Valley, CA 91100 to 6024
                 Family Circle, Twin Fjords, MN 31415.
                 Please update your records to reflect this change of
                 address.
                 Sincerely,



  ⊔⊔⊔⊔⊔⊔⊔⊔1[s⊔⊔T⊔⊔⊔2⊔⊔⊔T⊔⊔⊔3⊔⊔⊔T▊⊔⊔4⊔⊔⊔T⊔⊔⊔5⊔⊔⊔⊔⊔⊔6⊔⊔⊔⊔⊔7⊔⊔⊔⊔⊔⊔
  COA492.LTR      ▊                  Num        0 % 26  Line 6 of Page 1 of 1
  Move the cursor to the place you want the text copied, then press F10.
  Esc-Exit                                              F10-Continue
```

Figure 18-3. Type/Edit screen for positioning copied text block.

5. Write duplicates the text block, inserts the copy in your document, and leaves the cursor on the first character of the copy.

107

To insert another copy of the text block elsewhere in your document, move the cursor to the new location and simultaneously press Shift and F7. You can continue to insert copies of the text block until you copy or move a different one.

Moving a Block of Text

When you move a block of text, you delete it from one location in the document and insert it into another. To move a text block:

1. From the Block operations submenu, select **M - Move**.

2. Write displays your document on the Type/Edit screen shown in Figure 18-4.

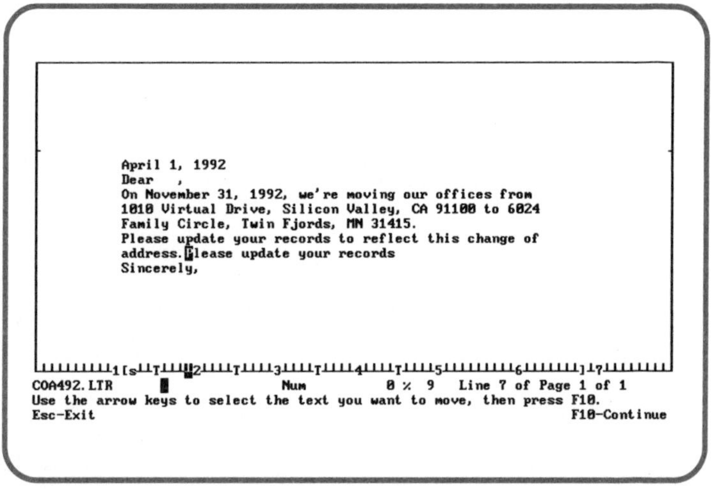

```
April 1, 1992
Dear    ,
On November 31, 1992, we're moving our offices from
1010 Virtual Drive, Silicon Valley, CA 91100 to 6024
Family Circle, Twin Fjords, MN 31415.
Please update your records to reflect this change of
address.▓lease update your records
Sincerely,
```

```
|||||||||||1[s||T|||||2|||||T|||3||||T||||4|||T||||5|||||||||6|||||||||17|||||||
COA492.LTR       ■                 Num          0 % 9    Line 7 of Page 1 of 1
Use the arrow keys to select the text you want to move, then press F10.
Esc-Exit                                                          F10-Continue
```

Figure 18-4. Type/Edit screen for selecting text block to move.

3. Press the arrow keys to highlight the rest of the text you want to move and then press F10.

4. After Write displays your document on the Type/ Edit screen shown in Figure 18-5, position the cursor where you want the first character of the moved text block inserted and press F10.

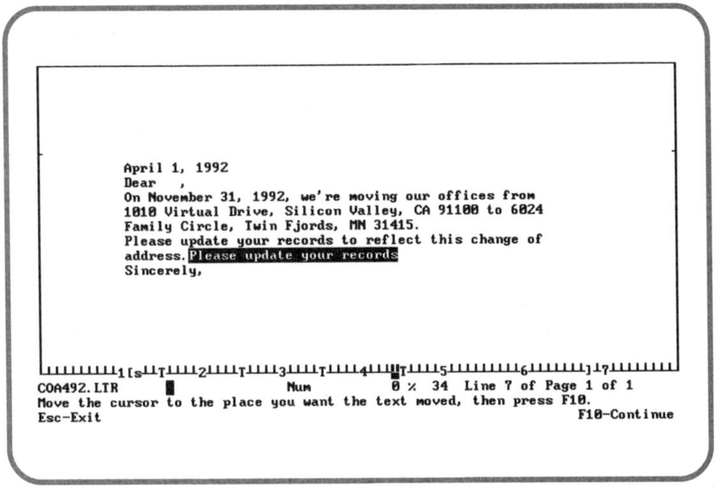

```
                April 1, 1992
                Dear   ,
                On November 31, 1992, we're moving our offices from
                1010 Virtual Drive, Silicon Valley, CA 91100 to 6024
                Family Circle, Twin Fjords, MN 31415.
                Please update your records to reflect this change of
                address. Please update your records
                Sincerely,




  LLLLLLLLLL1[s┴┴T┴┴┴2┴┴┴T┴┴┴3┴┴┴T┴┴┴4┴┴┴T┴┴┴5┴┴┴┴┴┴┴┴┴6┴┴┴┴┴┴]7┴┴┴┴┴┴
  COA492.LTR       ▌           Num           0 %  34  Line 7 of Page 1 of 1
  Move the cursor to the place you want the text moved, then press F10.
  Esc-Exit                                                      F10-Continue
```

Figure 18-5. Type/Edit screen for positioning moved text block.

5. Write deletes the text block, inserts it where you specified, and leaves the cursor on the first character of the moved block.

To insert a copy of the text block you just moved somewhere else in your document, move the cursor to the new location and simultaneously press Shift and F7. You can continue to insert copies of the moved text block until you copy or move a different one.

Copying and moving blocks of text are common editorial tasks. See the "Table of Features" at the back of this book for other ways you can quickly manipulate text blocks with the **B - Block operations** selection from the Options Menu.

In this lesson you've learned the principles of using the **B - Block operations** selection, and how to quickly select, copy, and move blocks of text. The next lesson describes how to apply typographical enhancements to text, set page breaks, and specify headers.

Lesson 19

Enhancing Text and Customizing Page Format

In this lesson, you'll learn how to enhance your document typographically, specify explicit page breaks, and set up document headers.

Bold, Italics, and Underline

Write lets you apply a variety of typographical enhancements to text. However, the type styles, weights, and individual fonts you can specify are limited to those your printer supports. The simplest way to enhance a block of text (for example, underline, italicize, or make boldface) involves these basic steps:

1. On the Type/Edit screen, move the cursor to the first character you want to select and press F8 to display the Options Menu.

2. Select **B - Block operations** to display the Block operations submenu (refer back to Figure 18-1).

3. Press → to move the highlight to the submenu and select **E - Enhance**.

4. When Write displays the Text Enhancements and Fonts Menu pictured in Figure 19-1, select an enhancement like **B - Bold**.

111

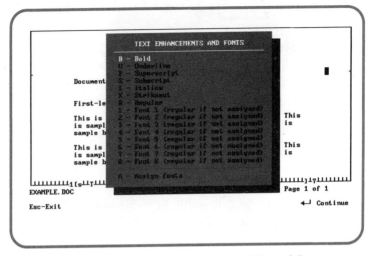

Figure 19-1. Text Enhancements and Fonts Menu.

5. Write displays your document on the Type/Edit screen shown in Figure 19-2, and prompts you to highlight the rest of the text you want to enhance.

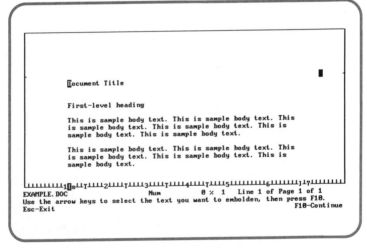

Figure 19-2. Type/Edit screen for selecting text block to enhance.

6. Press F10 when you've finished highlighting the block of text.

If your printer supports the enhancement you selected, Write applies it to the text block, highlights the enhanced text or displays it in color depending on your monitor's capabilities, and shows the name of the enhancement on the status line as illustrated in Figure 19-3.

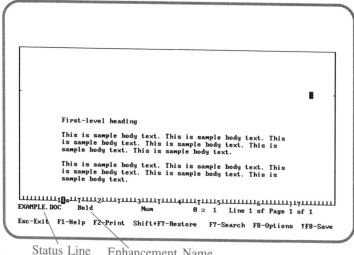

Status Line   Enhancement Name

Figure 19-3. Sample Type/Edit screen after enhancing text.

Setting Page Breaks

When your document contains material, such as a table, that you want to keep together on a page, you can specify a page break by following these steps:

1. On the Type/Edit screen, select the *first* line to print on the *new* page by moving the cursor anywhere on the line, and pressing F8 to display the Options Menu.

113

2. Press → to move the highlight to the submenu and select **N - Newpage**.

3. Write inserts its *newpage* code (shown in Figure 19-4) in your document and refreshes the Type/Edit screen to display the first line you selected and the text that follows it. To view the newpage code, press Page Up to display the text on the previous page.

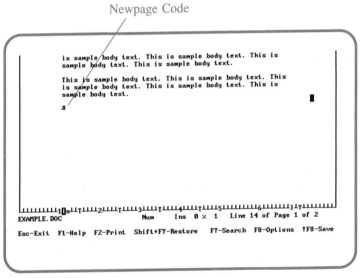

Newpage Code

Figure 19-4. Sample Type/Edit screen with newpage code.

Newpage Code When you embed a *newpage code* in a document, the text that precedes it always ends on one page and the text that follows it always starts on a new page.

To cancel the page break, position the cursor on the newpage code and press Delete.

Adding Page Breaks Wait until you've finished writing, editing, and formatting a document before specifying page breaks; extensive editing can change your page break requirements.

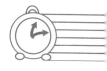

Adding a Header

You can add a header containing information such as chapter title, page number, date, and other text to your document. Because Write prints headers in the top margin, the margin must be large enough to accommodate your header text. Refer to Lesson 17 for details on setting margins with the Define Page screen.

Header A *header* is any information that you want to print on every page in the top margin of your document.

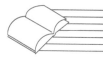

To add a header to your document:

1. From the Type/Edit screen, press F8 to display the Options Menu.

2. Press → to move the highlight to the submenu and select **H - Edit Header**.

3. Write displays the header window at the top of the screen (illustrated in Figure 19-5) with the cursor in the window's first character position.

4. Type the text for the header just as you would type in document text on the Type/Edit screen.

5. Press F10 when you've finished.

Write displays the Type/Edit screen with the header at the top of the screen.

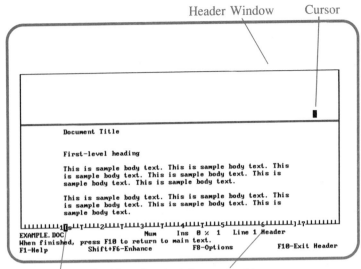

Header Window   Cursor

Horizontal Cursor Position   Vertical Cursor Position

Figure 19-5. Type/Edit screen with header window.

The following example shows how to add a simple header that includes some of Write's special options:

1. With the cursor in the header window, type the title of your document and a space.

2. Then type ***@DATE(1)* *@TIME(1)* Page #** and press F10.

Figure 19.6 illustrates a sample header derived and printed from this specification. When you use

@DATE(1)	Write automatically substitutes the date on which you saved this version of the document, and displays it in date format **1** (of 4).
@TIME(1)	Write automatically substitutes the time at which you saved this version of the

document, and displays it in time format **1** (of 3).

Write displays the current page number.

Text You Entered

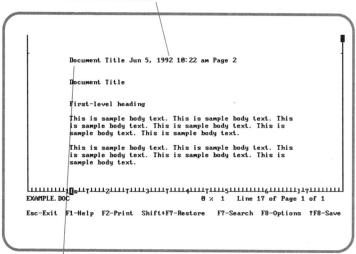

Title of Your Document

Figure 19-6. Sample header.

Simple headers that automatically display page numbers and time stamps are particularly useful when you're drafting or revising a document.

Table 19-1 summarizes date and time formats.

Table 19-1. Date and time formats

Format	Date/time sample display
1	Dec 22, 1992
	5:08 pm
2	22 Dec 1992
	17:08

117

Table 19-1. (continued)

Format	Date/time sample display
3	12/22/92
	17.08
4	22/12/92

In addition to specifying repeating headers, you can also set up repeating footers for your document. See the "Table of Features" at the back of this book for text enhancements and other options you can apply to headers and footers.

In this lesson, you've learned how to enhance text, set page breaks, and add a header to your document. The next lesson describes Write's search and replace functions.

Lesson 20

Using Search and Replace

In this lesson, you'll learn the basics of using Write's search and replace functions.

Using Search

When you're writing, editing, or formatting a document, you can use Write's search function to

- Quickly move the cursor elsewhere in your text by searching for a unique word or phrase

- Find all occurrences of a particular word, partial word, phrase, embedded formatting code, or character pattern

- Locate each occurrence of a particular word, and view and edit its use in context

The quickest way to get the most out of Write's search function is to invoke it, display its Advanced Options menu, and make selections appropriate to the kind of search you want to make. The following steps outline the basics of specifying search options:

1. From the Type/Edit screen, press F7 to display the Search for: box shown in Figure 20-1.

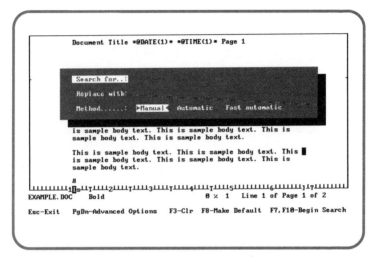

Figure 20-1. Search for: box.

2. Type in the character string or pattern for which you want to search.

Character String A character string is any partial word, entire word, phrase, or set of alphanumeric characters, punctuation, and blank spaces.

Pattern A pattern is a particular grouping of characters; for example, telephone numbers or zip codes.

3. Press Page Down to display the Advanced Options menu pictured in Figure 20-2.

4. With the mouse or the arrow keys, move the highlight bar to any option you need to change and make a selection appropriate to your search. Search options and their functions are described in the next section.

5. Press F7 to start your search or press Esc to cancel it.

Keeping Search Defaults If you want to do a number of searches of the same kind, press F8 to make your selections the default search options.

```
        Document Title *@DATE(1)* *@TIME(1)* Page 1

    Search for..: text
    Replace with:
    Method......: ►Manual◄  Automatic  Fast automatic
    Type........: ►Whole words◄  Text  Pattern
    Case........: ►Insensitive◄  Sensitive
    Range.......: ►All◄  To end  To beginning
    Search Joins: Yes ►No◄

⊥⊥⊥⊥⊥⊥⊥1[s⊥⊥7⊥⊥⊥2⊥⊥⊥7⊥⊥⊥3⊥⊥⊥7⊥⊥⊥4⊥⊥⊥7⊥⊥⊥5⊥⊥⊥⊥⊥⊥⊥6⊥⊥⊥⊥⊥⊥7⊥⊥⊥⊥⊥
EXAMPLE.DOC    Bold                    0 % 1    Line 1 of Page 1 of 2

Esc-Exit    PgUp-Reg Options    F3-Clear    F8-Make Default    F7,F10-Begin Search
```

Figure 20-2. Advanced Options menu.

Search Options

This section introduces you to the search options available on the Advanced Options menu.

Method Option

Manual Stops at each match and prompts you to press F7 again to continue the search; appropriate for quickly moving the cursor to a new location or viewing and editing text in context.

121

Match A match is any occurrence of the character string or pattern for which you're searching that also matches the search options you've specified.

Automatic   Reports the number of matches; appropriate for counting occurrences.

Fast Automatic Same as **Automatic**.

Type Option

Whole words   Matches only complete words that correspond to the character string for which you're searching (for example, searching for *one* finds *one* and *One*, but doesn't find a match with *alone*, *clone*, or *telephone*); appropriate for narrowing a search.

Text   Matches any character string that corresponds to the one you specified (for example, searching for *work* also finds *worker* and *workplace*); appropriate for searching for all forms of a word, all occurrences of embedded formatting codes (for example, **@it** for italics), or other sets of arbitrary characters.

Pattern   Matches a group of characters that corresponds to the pattern you specified; appropriate for telephone numbers, zip codes, or other uniform sequences. For example, searching for the pattern **???~???~????** locates all telephone numbers with area codes. The **?** (question mark) stands for any alphanumeric character and the ~ (tilde) represents any nonalphanumeric character separator.

Case Option

Insensitive   Finds a match when any string of upper- and lowercase characters (corresponds) to the one you specified; appropriate for locating all occurrences of a character string.

Sensitive   Finds a match only when upper- and lowercase characters precisely correspond to the character string for which you're searching; appropriate for narrowing a search.

Range Option

All   Searches the entire document starting from the current cursor position; appropriate for most searches (because you might forget about something you did earlier or not know about text someone else added to the document).

To end   Searches from the current cursor position to the last character position in the document.

To beginning   Searches from the current cursor position to the first character position in the document.

Search Joins Option

Yes	Searches through all documents connected (by Q&A commands) to the document on the Type/Edit screen.
No	Confines search to the document on Type/Edit screen.

Replace Options

You can use Write's search function to locate a particular character string, and replace it with another by following these steps:

1. From the Type/Edit screen, press F7 to display the Search for: box shown in Figure 20-1.

2. Type in the character string for which you want to search.

3. Move the cursor to the Replace with: field and type in the text you want to replace the character string for which you're searching.

4. For the Method option, select Manual to stop at each match and confirm its replacement by pressing F10, or revoke its replacement by pressing F7.

   Select Automatic to make replacements without your explicit confirmation; Write displays each replacement as it makes it.

   Select Fast Automatic to make replacements without your explicit confirmation; Write does not display replacements as they're made.

5. Follow steps 3 and 4 described in "Using Search" to specify the other search options.

6. Press F7 to begin searching and replacing. To cancel the operation press Esc. Any replacements made before you press Esc remain intact.

Using the Manual Option Because search and replace are powerful functions, it's a good idea to use the **Manual** search option until you get familiar with searching for and replacing text. You might not anticipate all the matches a search will locate, and the **Manual** search option gives you the opportunity to stop a replacement.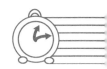

In this lesson, you've learned the basics of using the word processor's search and replace functions. The next lesson covers printing a document.

Printing a Document

In this lesson, you'll learn how to print a document from Write. You'll also get some tips for making your documents look more professional.

Printing Your Document

To print a document with Write, the text must be displayed on the Type/Edit screen. If it's not, follow steps 1 and 2; otherwise start with step 3:

1. Select **W - Write** from the Main Menu.

2. Retrieve your document as described in "Getting a Document" in Lesson 16.

3. From the Type/Edit screen, press Ctrl and F6 simultaneously to display the Define Page Menu pictured in Figure 21-1.

4. Make any changes appropriate for your document and press F10 to return to it.

5. If you want to save changes you made to the Define Page Menu, simultaneously press Shift and F8, and

then press Enter after Write displays the Save as: box.

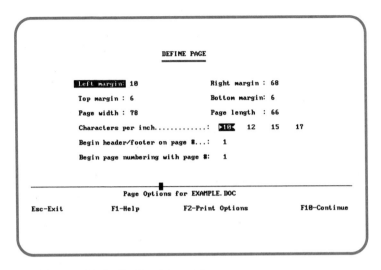

Figure 21-1. Define Page Menu.

6. Press F2 to display the Print Options Menu shown in Figure 21-2, and make any necessary changes. (Press F1 and then Page Down to display the help screens for Write's printing options.)

7. Press F10 to print your document.

Options Menu Formatting Tips

While you're entering or editing a document on the Type/ Edit screen, you can specify typographical formatting by selecting **B - Block operations** from the Options Menu and **E - Enhance** from its submenu. (Enhancing a document is covered in Lesson 19.) You can make your documents look more professional if you do the following things:

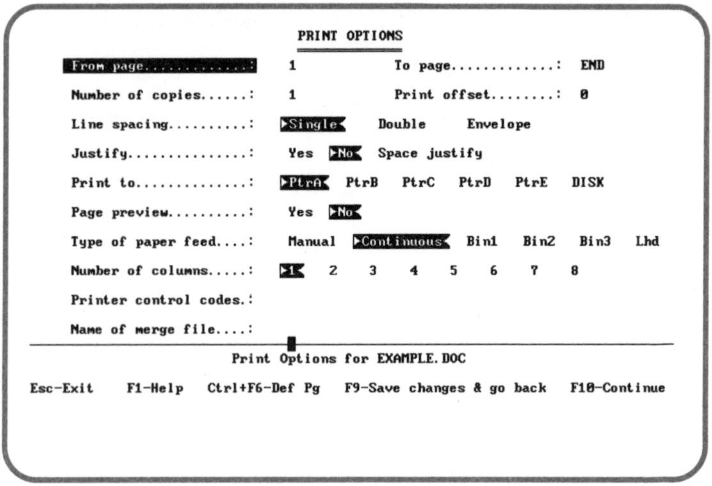

```
                    PRINT OPTIONS
   From page............:   1              To page............:   END
   Number of copies......:  1              Print offset........:   0
   Line spacing.........:  >Single<   Double      Envelope
   Justify..............:   Yes  >No<  Space justify
   Print to.............:  >PtrA<  PtrB   PtrC   PtrD   PtrE   DISK
   Page preview.........:   Yes  >No<
   Type of paper feed....:  Manual  >Continuous<  Bin1   Bin2   Bin3   Lhd
   Number of columns.....:  >1<  2   3   4   5   6   7   8
   Printer control codes.:
   Name of merge file....:       ▮
   ─────────────────────────────────────────────────────────────────
                    Print Options for EXAMPLE.DOC

 Esc-Exit    F1-Help   Ctrl+F6-Def Pg   F9-Save changes & go back   F10-Continue
```

Figure 21-2. Print Options Menu.

- Avoid using more than two fonts; rather than enhancing a document, many different fonts distract the reader and make text harder to read. A good rule of thumb is to use one font for body text and the other for headings.

- Reserve italics for emphasis, foreign words, or citing documents by title (its normal uses).

- Put one blank space after closing punctuation when using proportional fonts. Two blanks are appropriate only for monospaced fonts like those found on a standard typewriter.

- Be consistent with your conventions in reports or larger documents; for example, all first-level headings should look the same and be distinct from second-level headings.

Define Page Menu Formatting Tips

When setting margins with the Define Page Menu, remember the value of white space. Trying to fit too much type on a page detracts from your document's appearance and can intimidate readers. As a general rule, set left and right margins to

- 1 inch for body text in 12 point monospaced fonts like Courier or 10 pitch typewriter fonts

- 1.75 inches for body text in 12 point proportional fonts like Times Roman

With the Define Page Menu, you can also specify the page on which headers, footers, and page numbers start printing by simply typing in the number of the page. Standard convention is to start printing these elements on the second page of a document.

Setting margins is described in Lesson 17 and adding headers is covered in Lesson 19.

Print Options Menu Formatting Tips

The Print Options Menu lets you specify line spacing and justification. Single spacing is appropriate for finished documents. Double-spacing is convenient for drafts and documents you intend to circulate for review and comments.

For the Justify option, selecting **Yes** aligns text with both the left and right margins. **No** aligns text with only the left margin. Full justification is appropriate for body text in a proportional font. However, justifying text in a monospaced font usually makes it hard to read because blanks inserted to stretch out a line to the right margin often create distracting "rivers" of white space.

For descriptions of other printing options, see Table 14-2 "Report Print Options."

In this lesson, you've learned to use Write to print a document and have reviewed some formatting tips. The next lesson shows you how to print mailing labels.

Lesson 22

Printing
Mailing Labels

In this lesson, you'll learn how to print mailing labels
with information from your database.

Mailing Label Templates

Q&A comes with a set of predefined templates for many
standard mailing labels and printers. You can copy and
modify these templates to print names and addresses retrieved from one of your databases as follows. Making a
copy of the template and tailoring it for a particular database preserves the original template definition for future
use.

1. Select **M - Mailing labels** from the Write Menu to
   display the List of Mailing Labels screen shown in
   Figure 22-1.

2. Move the highlight to the label that most closely
   matches the one you want, and press F5 to make a
   copy of the template.

3. With the cursor to the right of the `Copy to:`
   prompt that Write displays, type a name containing
   no more than 32 characters and press F10.

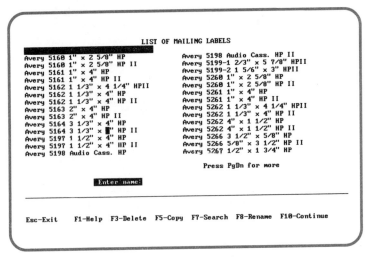

Figure 22-1. List of Mailing Labels screen.

Write saves your copy and enters the name you typed in the alphabetical list of labels, as shown in Figure 22-2. Select the name of your copy from this list to display its generic field labels on a screen similar to the one in Figure 22-3. Use the following steps to create your own custom field labels.

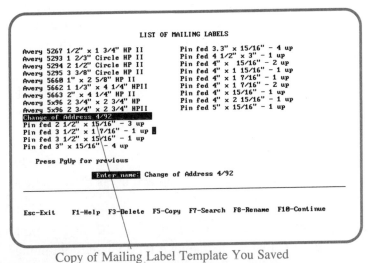

Copy of Mailing Label Template You Saved

Figure 22-2. Alphabetical mailing label list.

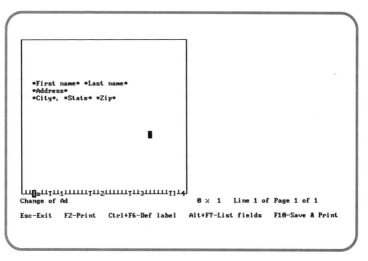

Figure 22-3. Copy of mailing label template with generic field labels.

1. Use the Backspace or Delete keys to remove any field labels you don't want.

2. Position the cursor where you want to insert a field label from your database.

3. Press Alt and F7 to display the Data file name: box and press Enter.

4. Select your database from the list that Write displays. Write displays your database's field labels as shown in Figure 22-4.

5. Move the highlight to a field label you want to add to your mailing label and press Enter.

Write inserts your field label within asterisks at the cursor position in the mailing label. Continue to modify your mailing label by positioning the cursor for the next field label to be inserted, pressing Alt and F7 to display database field labels, selecting one, and inserting it in the mailing label. To save your mailing label:

133

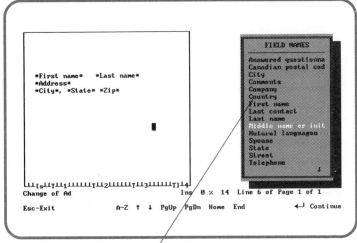

Your Database Field Labels

Figure 22-4. Copy of mailing label template with database's field labels.

- Press Shift and F8 simultaneously.

Using the Options Menu Press F8 to display Write's Options Menu and use it to modify your mailing label. Refer to Lessons 17 through 19 for details on editing options.

When you are ready to print your labels, simultaneously press Ctrl and F6 to display the Define Label screen (shown in Figure 22-5). Change the label dimensions if necessary and press F10. Follow these steps to print the labels:

1. Press F10 to display the Mailing Label Print Options screen pictured in Figure 22-6.

2. Specify options for your system, and press F10. (Press F1 and then Page Down to display the help screens.)

134

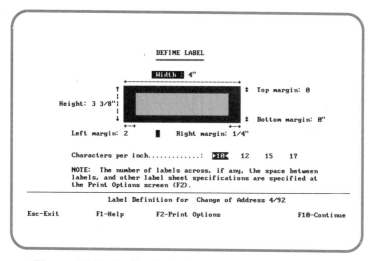

Figure 22-5. Define Label screen.

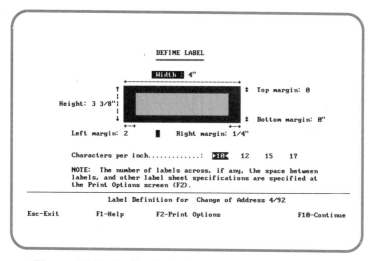

Figure 22-6. Mailing Label Print Options screen.

3. After you've selected print options, Write displays the retrieve spec for your database. Fill it in (refer to Lesson 6 for information on retrieving records) and press F10.

135

4. Write prompts you to press Enter to print your labels or Esc to cancel the operation.

In this lesson, you've learned how to print database information on mailing labels with Write. The next lesson shows you how to merge data from a database with text in a document.

Lesson 23

Merging Data with Text in a Document

In this lesson, you'll learn how to create a document and merge database information into the document you create. You'll also learn the basics of formatting and printing the merged document.

Creating the Document

Q&A makes it easy for you to draft a document and intergrate information from your databases. For example, you might want to send a form letter announcing an impending change of address to individuals whose names and addresses are stored in one of your databases. First, you need to use Write to create the document (described in Lessons 15 through 21).

To set up a document to incorporate the name and address of individual recipients retrieved from your database, the document must be displayed on Write's Type/Edit screen. To display the document,

1. Select **W - Write** from the Main Menu.

2. Retrieve your document as described in "Getting a Document" in Lesson 16.

To specify where in the document to print information from the database, follow these steps:

1. Place the cursor where you want to insert the data from a particular field (for example, the First name: field), and press Alt and F7 to display the Data file name: box.

2. Press the space bar and Enter, and then select the name of the database from the list Write displays.

3. Write displays the database's field names, as shown in Figure 23-1. Move the highlight to the field name you want to insert in your document and press Enter.

4. Write inserts the field name within asterisks at the cursor position in the document.

5. Continue to modify your document by positioning the cursor for the next field name to be inserted, pressing Alt and F7 to display field names, selecting one, and inserting it in the document.

Selecting Options Press F8 to display Write's Options Menu and use the options to modify your document. Refer to Lessons 17 through 19 for details on editing options.

6. When you've finished inserting field names, press Shift and F8 to display the Save as: box. Type in a new document file name (containing no more than eight characters) for your form letter and press Enter; or simply press Enter to save your form letter with the name of your draft document.

Formatting the Merged Data

When you specify a field to be merged with a document, the data from the field prints as it exists in the database.

Sometimes that field contains blank spaces that are inappropriate for the context in which you want the field information to display in your document. To trim extraneous spaces, type (**T**) between the field name and the asterisk following it. Other formatting options are available from the Write Options Menu, which you can display by pressing F8.

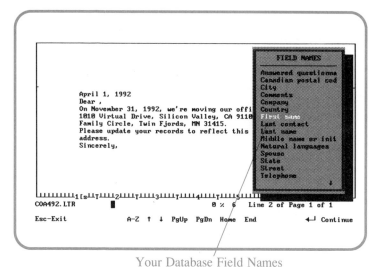

Your Database Field Names

Figure 23-1. Screen with database field names.

Printing a Merged Document

To print your document with information retrieved from your database, the document must be on the Type/Edit screen. To print the document:

1. If the Type/Edit screen is not displayed, select W - Write from the Main Menu.

2. Retrieve your document as described in "Getting a Document" in Lesson 16.

139

3. Press Ctrl and F6 to display the Define Page screen (shown in Figure 23-2). Change the specifications as necessary and press F10.

4. Press F2 to display the Print Options screen pictured in Figure 23-3; then specify options for your system and press F10. (Press F1 and then Page Down to display the help screens.)

5. After you've selected print options, Write displays the retrieve spec for your database. Fill it in (refer to Lesson 6 for information on retrieving records), and press F8 to display the sort spec screen.

6. Make your sorting specifications (refer to Lesson 7) and press F10.

7. Write displays a confirmation message. Press Enter to print your document with information merged from the database, or press Esc to cancel printing and return to the Type\Edit screen.

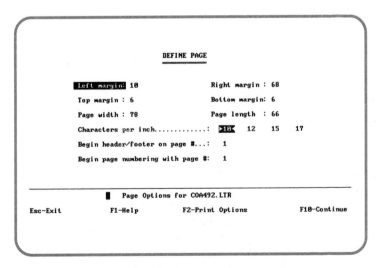

Figure 23-2. Define Page screen.

```
                         PRINT OPTIONS
                         ─────────────
   From page............:    1              To page.............:   END

   Number of copies......:    1          Print offset........:    0

   Line spacing.........:   ▶Single◀   Double     Envelope

   Justify..............:   Yes  ▶No◀  Space justify

   Print to.............:   ▶PtrA◀  PtrB    PtrC    PtrD    PtrE    DISK

   Page preview.........:   Yes  ▶No◀

   Type of paper feed...:   Manual  ▶Continuous◀  Bin1    Bin2    Bin3    Lhd

   Number of columns.....:  ▶1◀   2    3    4    5    6    7    8

   Printer control codes.:

   Name of merge file....:   C:\QA\ADRSBOOK.DTF
   ──────────────────────────────────────────────────────────────────
              ▮    Print Options for COA492.LTR

Esc-Exit    F1-Help   Ctrl+F6-Def Pg   F9-Save changes & go back   F10-Continue
```

Figure 23-3. Print Options screen.

Q&A has additional facilities for formatting field information and for embedding programming expressions in documents in which data is merged. For a list of these features, see the Table of Features at the back of this book.

In this lesson, you've learned the basics of creating, formatting, and printing a document in which you've merged information from your database.

Specifying Printers

Before you can print data from Q&A, you must specify a printer as follows:

1. Start Q&A following the instructions in Lesson 2.

2. Select **U - Utilities** from the Main Menu and **P - Install Printer** from the Utilities Menu.

3. Q&A displays the Printer Selection screen shown in Figure SP-1.

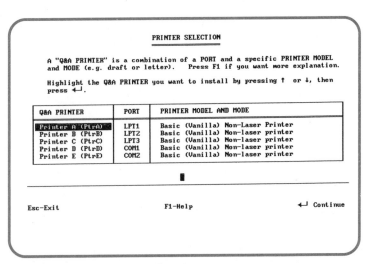

Figure SP-1. Printer Selection screen.

4. The selections in the Q&A Printer column are simply a list of the names that you can assign to the printers attached to your computer. Select **Printer A (PtrA)**.

5. When Q&A displays the Port Selection screen shown in Figure SP-2, select the port to which your printer is attached.

Port Port refers to the connector to which the printer cable is attached at the back of your computer.

If you have only one printer installed, your printer port is probably LPT1. Consult your computer manual or the back of your computer for the correct port to select.

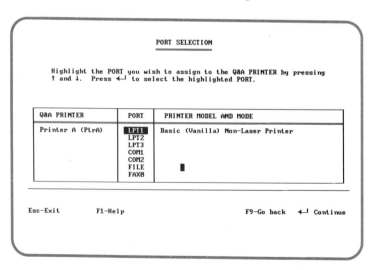

```
                          PORT SELECTION
                          ════════════

        Highlight the PORT you wish to assign to the Q&A PRINTER by pressing
        ↑ and ↓.  Press ←┘ to select the highlighted PORT.


        ┌──────────────────┬─────────┬────────────────────────────────────┐
        │ Q&A PRINTER      │ PORT    │ PRINTER MODEL AND MODE             │
        ├──────────────────┼─────────┼────────────────────────────────────┤
        │ Printer A (PtrA) │ LPT1    │ Basic (Vanilla) Non-Laser Printer  │
        │                  │ LPT2    │                                    │
        │                  │ LPT3    │                                    │
        │                  │ COM1    │                                    │
        │                  │ COM2    │ ▮                                  │
        │                  │ FILE    │                                    │
        │                  │ FAX0    │                                    │
        └──────────────────┴─────────┴────────────────────────────────────┘


    Esc-Exit        F1-Help                      F9-Go back  ←┘ Continue
```

Figure SP-2. Port Selection screen.

6. When Q&A displays the List of Printer Manufacturers screen shown in Figure SP-3, select your printer's manufacturer. If the manufacturer isn't on the list, select **Basic (Vanilla)**.

143

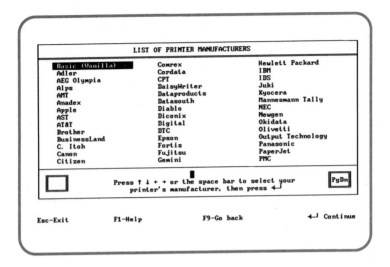

Figure SP-3. List of Printer Manufacturers screen.

7. Q&A displays a list of your manufacturer's printers that it can support. Select the name of the one that is attached to your computer.

8. Q&A then displays a box describing which printer you have specified and any special requirements (such as font cartridges) it has for certain types of printing. Press Enter to confirm your specification or Esc to return to the list of printers.

9. Once you've confirmed your specification, Q&A displays a message asking if you want to install another printer.

10. Select **Y - Yes** if you want to install another printer and repeat the process starting with step 3. Otherwise, select **N - No** to return to the Utilities Menu and Esc to return to the Main Menu.

Q&A 4.0 Table of Features

Feature	Description	Menu
Database Features		
Access to SQL	Retrieve and manipulate data from Structured Query Language tables	File
Copy	Duplicate when adding data	
	From same field of previous record	File
	From all fields of previous record	File
	Copy database design, Intelligent Assistant/ Query Guide, and/or selected records to another database	File
Cross-tab reports	Summarize and cross-reference data by row, column, and summary fields	Report
Custom help screens	Define custom help screens	File
Custom menus	Customize Q&A menus for your installation	File
Database design	Design and format database form	File
Database security	Set user IDs, passwords, and access rights for single- and multiuser databases	File
Field restriction	Control data entry with =, >, or < restrictions	File
Field templates	Display form format to guide data entry for account numbers and so on	File

Feature	Description	Menu
Intelligent Assistant/ Query Guide	Retrieve and report data with natural language interface; with IA, ask questions comparing different parts of a database, follow-up questions without retyping	Assistant
Import/Export	Import/export data in pfs/Professional File; IBM Filing Asst; Lotus 1-2-3/Symphony; dBase II, III, IV; and Paradox formats	File
Information types	Set field data type to date, hours, keyword, money, number, text, yes/no	File
Input formatting	Insert commas, justify, and change text case during data entry	File
Post	Send data from one database to another	File
Print	Form and records Reports	File Report
Program database	Program database form to verify data entry, do calculations, and look up values	File
Redesign database	Change format and form	File
Save specs	Name and save data retrieval, sorting, merging, updating, importing, exporting, and report printing specifications	File
Spell check	Check field data spelling when adding or updating	File
Thesaurus	Give synonyms for field data when adding or updating	File

Feature	Description	Menu
Utilities	Specify printers; modify font description files; access DOS file functions; specify directory paths, automatic execution, and network IDs; install Main menu selections for alternate programs	Utilities

Write Features

Feature	Description	Menu
Capitalize text	Change text block to uppercase	None
Capitalize titles	Capitalize acronyms and first letter of non-prepositions in text block	None
Copy text	Copy text block to disk under a specified file name	None
Document recovery	Restore damaged document files	Write
Enhance text format	Specify type weight, style, and font for text block	None
Header/Footer	Specify running headers/ footers	Write
Import/Export	Import/Export documents in ASCII, Mac ASCII, DCA, WordStar, WordPerfect, Microsoft Word, Multimate, or Professional Write format	Write
Lowercase text	Change text block to lowercase	
Mail merge	Insert database information into form letters and mailing labels	Write
Move text to file	Move text block to disk under a specified file name (deletes text from original location)	None

147

Feature	Description	Menu
Print text block	Print text block	None
Program mail merge	Embed programming statements in form letters to generate custom calculations or look up database information	Write
Search/Replace	Search text by word, character string, or pattern and optionally replace matches with another string	Write
Spell check	Check spelling when writing or editing a document	Write
Thesaurus	Give synonyms when writing or editing a document	Write

DOS Primer

This section highlights some of the DOS procedures you will use during your work with this program.

DOS is your computer's Disk Operating System. It functions as a go-between program that lets the various components of your computer system talk with one another. Whenever you type anything using your keyboard, whenever you move your mouse, whenever you try to print a file, DOS interprets the commands and coordinates the task. The following sections explain how to run DOS on your computer and what you can expect to see.

Changing Disk Drives

You must have a hard disk and PC/MS DOS 2.0 or higher (DOS 3.3 for PS/2 model computers) installed on it to run Q&A 4.0. When you turn on your computer, DOS automatically loads and displays a prompt (also known as the DOS prompt) that looks something like **C:\>**. This prompt tells you which disk drive is currently active. Your hard disk drive is usually labeled C. (Most computers have only one hard disk, but it may be treated as several disk drives:

149

C, D, E, F, and so on.) The floppy disk drives, the drives located on the front of your computer, are drives A and B. If you have only one floppy drive, it's usually A and you have no drive B. If you have two floppy drives, the top or left drive is usually A, and the bottom or right drive is B. You can activate a different drive at any time by performing the following steps:

1. Make sure there's a formatted disk in the drive you want to activate.

2. Type the letter of the drive followed by a colon. For example, type a:.

3. Press Enter. The DOS prompt changes to show that the drive you selected is now active.

Using DISKCOPY to Make Backups of the Q&A Program Disks

Before you install Q&A on your hard disk, you should make backup copies of the original program disks. By using backups to install or run the program, you avoid the risk of damaging the original disks.

Obtain 7 blank 5.25" double-sided double-density disks or 4 blank 3.5" double-sided double-density disks. The type of disk should be marked on the package. Because the DISKCOPY command copies the entire disk, you don't have to format the blank disks before you begin

1. Change to the drive that contains the DOS program files.

2. If the DISKCOPY file is in a separate directory, change to that directory as explained earlier. For

example, if the file is in the C:\DOS directory, type cd\dos at the C:> prompt, and press Enter.

3. Type diskcopy a: a: or diskcopy b: b:, depending on which drive you're using to make the copies.

4. Press Enter. A message appears, telling you to insert the source diskette into the floppy drive.

5. Insert the original Q&A disk you want to copy into drive A and press Enter. DOS copies the disk into RAM (Random Access Memory). When DOS is done copying the original disk, a message appears telling you to insert the target diskette into the floppy drive.

6. Insert one of the blank disks into the floppy drive, and press Enter. DOS copies the disk from RAM onto the blank disk. When the copying is complete, a message appears, asking if you want to copy another diskette.

7. Remove the disk from the drive, and label it with the same name and number that appears on the original disk.

8. If you need to copy another original disk, type y and go back to step 5. Continue until you copy all the original disks.

9. When you're done copying disks, type n when asked if you want to copy another disk.

10. Put the original disks back in their box and store them in a safe place.

Formatting Floppy Disks

The first step in preparing floppy disks to store programs and data is formatting the disks.

What Is Formatting? The formatting procedure creates a map on the disk that later tells DOS where to find the information you store on the disk. You cannot place any information—programs or data of any kind—on a new disk before the disk is formatted. Formatting also erases any information on a diskette. Do not format your hard disk drive, however, because formatting a hard disk erases all programs and information on the hard disk.

1. Turn on your computer.

2. Change to the drive and directory that contains your DOS files. For example, if your DOS files are in C:\DOS, type **cd\dos** at the C:\> prompt and press Enter.

3. Insert the blank floppy disk you want to format in the A or B drive.

4. Type **format a:** or **format b:** and press Enter. The system prompts you to insert the disk (which you've already done).

5. Press Enter. The system then begins formatting the disk. When formatting is complete, the system asks whether you want to format another.

6. Type **y** if you want to format additional disks, then repeat all steps. Otherwise, type **n** to quit.

Labeling Disks While the disk is being formatted, you may want to use the time to write the
labels for the disks. Be sure to write on the
labels before you attach them to the diskettes.
(If you've already placed the labels on the
diskettes, write on the labels using a felt-tip pen.
The hard point of a ball-point pen can damage
the surface of a diskette.)

Working with Directories

Because hard drives hold much more information than
floppy drives, hard drives are usually divided into directories. For example, when you install Q&A, the Installation
program suggests that you copy the Q&A program files to
a directory called \QA on drive C. This directory then
branches off from the root directory of drive C, keeping all
the Q&A program files separate from all the other files on
drive C. Directories can contain subdirectories as well.

Making Directories

To create a directory, you must use the MD (MAKE
DIRECTORY) command. Follow these steps:

1. Change to the drive that you want to contain the
   directory.

2. At the DOS prompt, type md*directoryname*.
   (Substitute the name for the directory you are
   creating in place of *directoryname*.)

3. Press Enter. The directory now exists off the root
   directory. If you want to create a subdirectory off a
   directory, type the directory name, a backslash and
   then a subdirectory name, and press Enter.

153

Note: You do not need to create a directory to run Q&A; the installation program takes care of this for you. However, you may want to create subdirectories in it for storing your document database and temporary files. See lesson 15 for instructions on using **S-Set global options** for storing files in subdirectories.

Moving to a Directory

You need to be able to move from directory to directory. To change directories, you must use the CD (CHANGE DIRECTORY) command:

1. Change to the drive that contains the directory.

2. At the DOS prompt, type cd*directoryname*. (For example, type cd\\qa.) The backslash (\\) you type tells DOS to begin at the root directory and move to the directory you specified under the root. Use the backslash to separate all directories and subdirectories in a command line. For example, to move to a subdirectory of a directory, the command line would look like this:

   cd*directoryname**subdirectoryname*

   This command line specifies a complete path to the subdirectory.

3. Press Enter.

Displaying Directory Contents

To see which files are stored in a directory, use the DIR (DIRECTORY) command.

1. Change to the drive and directory whose contents you want to view.

2. Type **dir** and press Enter. A list of files appears.

If the list is too long to fit on the screen, it scrolls off the top. You can view the entire list by typing **/p** (pause) or **/w** (wide) after the DIR command. If you type **dir/p**, DOS displays one screenful of files; you can see the next screen by pressing any key. If you type **dir/w**, DOS displays the list across the screen, fitting many more file names on screen.

Working with Files

DOS also includes commands you can use to work with the files you create. This section briefly introduces the procedures for copying, deleting, and renaming files.

Copying Files

When you want to copy files using DOS, use the COPY command as follows:

1. Move to the directory that stores the file (or files) you want to copy.

2. Type the command line:

   copy *filename1 drive:\directoryname\filename2*

   In this command line, *filename1* is the name of the existing file you want to copy, *drive:\directoryname* is the drive and directory you want to copy the file to, and *filename2* is the new name you want to give the copy of the file. If you want to create a copy of the file in the same drive or directory, you can omit the path (*drive:\directoryname*) before *filename2*.

3. Press Enter. DOS copies the file and places the copy in the current directory.

Deleting Files

To delete files using DOS, you use the DELETE (DEL) command:

1. Move to the directory that stores the file you want to delete.

2. Type the command line:

   del *filename*

3. Press Enter. DOS deletes the file.

Renaming Files

Use the RENAME (REN) command to rename files in DOS:

1. Move to the directory that stores the file you want to rename.

2. Type the command line:

   rename *filename1 filename2*

   Or

   ren *filename1 filename2*

   In this command line, *filename1* is the name of the existing file, and *filename2* is the new name you want to assign to the file.

3. Press Enter. DOS renames the file and keeps it in the current directory.

For more information about using DOS commands, see *The First Book of MS-DOS.*

Index

specifying printers, 142-144
starting, 1
Table of Features, 145-148
updating databases, 43-49
using Ditto, 29-31
using Write's search and
replace, 119-125
working with blocks of Write
text, 105-110
Query Guide, 8-11,
quitting Q&A, 6

— **R** —

records
copying field information, 29-
31
correcting mistakes, 26-27
defined, 8
deleting, 43
editing, 43
editing in form view, 44-45
editing in table view, 46-47
entering data, 22-27
printing, 57
printing all, 58
printing entire, 62
retrieving, 32
retrieving a group of, 34-36
retrieving all, 33
retrieving specific, 33-36
selecting to include in report,
68-70
sorting, 39-42
viewing in form view, 9-11
viewing in table view, 9-13
redesigning
forms, 52-54
removing
error messages, 24

replacing
in documents, 124-125
reports
basic steps in creating, 64-70
columnar reports, 69
cross-tabular, 73-77
defining and saving a columnar report, 71
defining and saving cross-
tabular, 75-77
formatting, 78-84
printing, 80-84
saving columnar, 71
selecting records, 68-70
setting up columns and rows,
73-74
using sample, 68
retrieve spec
loading, 36
Retrieve Spec screen, 32-36
retrieve specs
saving, 35
retrieving
a group of records, 34-36
all records, 33
documents, 92-93
specific records, 33-36
rows
in cross-tabular reports, 73-74

— **S** —

saving
a retrieve spec, 35
data, 24-28
print specs, 59-61
sort specs, 40
Write documents, 89
search options, 121-124
searching
a document, 119-124